Dear Reader:

The book you are about to read is the latest bestseller from the St. Martin's True Crime Library, the imprint the *New York Times* calls "the leader in true crime!" Each month, we offer you a fascinating account of the latest, most sensational crime that has captured the national attention. St. Martin's is the publisher of perennial bestselling true crime author Jack Olsen, whose SALT OF THE EARTH is the true story of one woman's triumph over life-shattering violence; Joseph Wambaugh called it "powerful and absorbing." Fannie Weinstein and Melinda Wilson tell the story of a beautiful honors student who was lured into the hidden world of sex for hire in THE COED CALL GIRL MURDER. St. Martin's is also proud to publish two-time Edgar Award-winning author Carlton Stowers, whose TO THE LAST BREATH recounts a two-year-old girl's mysterious death, and the dogged investigation that led loved ones to the most unlikely murderer: her own father. The book you now hold, ANGELS OF DEATH by Gary C. King, looks at an amazing case that made national headlines.

St. Martin's True Crime Library gives you the stories *behind* the headlines. Our authors take you right to the scene of the crime and into the minds of the most notorious murderers to show you what really makes them tick. St. Martin's True Crime Library paperbacks are better than the most terrifying thriller, because it's all true! The next time you want a crackling good read, make sure it's got the St. Martin's True Crime Library logo on the spine—you'll be up all night!

Charles E. Spicer

Charles E. Spicer, Jr.
Executive Editor, St. Martin's True Crime Library

Finding the Victim

While the fire in the house was being extinguished, other fire-fighters went room-to-room searching for the house's inhabitants. Although it was only a few days after Thanksgiving, the fire investigators found a box of Christmas decorations as they entered another room. With Christmas less than a month away, it was obvious that the occupants had been getting ready to decorate their home.

It wasn't until the investigators closely examined the room at the east end of the house that they found anyone. There was a man sitting in a chair with his legs propped up on a sofa. The man was wearing shoes, pants and a camouflage jacket, and he had a coffee cup sitting beside his right leg between his leg and the chair. There was a *Lion King* pillow on the couch next to the man, indicating that a child or children might reside in the home with him . . .

When they first saw the man, the firefighters thought that he had been overcome by smoke and flames. However, upon closer examination, the firefighters observed that he had obvious injuries to his head, and they saw that there was considerable blood spatter on the walls around him . . .

St. Martin's Paperbacks
True Crime Library Titles
by Gary C. King

THE TEXAS 7
AN EARLY GRAVE
MURDER IN HOLLYWOOD
ANGELS OF DEATH

ANGELS OF DEATH

GARY C. KING

St. Martin's Paperbacks

ANGELS OF DEATH

ISBN: 0-312-98523-1

Printed in the United States of America

St. Martin's Paperbacks edition / September 2003

10 9 8 7 6 5 4 3 2 1

For my Father and Mother, Curtis and Eunice King,
who know the meaning of unconditional love.
Thanks for always being there.

Acknowledgments

A special thanks to Charles E. Spicer, Jr., executive editor at St. Martin's True Crime Library, for his enthusiasm in wanting to do this book and wanting to do this book with me. I am also indebted to his assistant editor, Joe Cleemann, who was very much as enthusiastic about the project and without whose skills this book would not have made it off the presses. I am especially grateful not only to Charles and Joe but to everyone at St. Martin's Paperbacks for their patience in seeing this project through to completion and for their caring and understanding through some very difficult times.

I am also grateful to Peter Miller, my agent, who, hopefully, hasn't given up on me yet! I couldn't do it without you in my corner, Peter. Thanks.

Also, much gratitude goes to Jorge Jaramillo at AP/Wide World for his assistance with the photos.

As always, I'm also grateful to Kirsten and Sarah for cheering me on when things get tough, but mostly for their undying love.

Special thanks to Brian Meehan, a good man I'm proud to call friend.

And finally, I am eternally grateful to my wonderful wife, Teresita, for sticking with me through thick and thin. Thanks for always being by my side, darlin'.

... Ye fathers, provoke not your children to wrath ...
—EPHESIANS 6:4

But the father answered never a word,
A frozen corpse was he.
—HENRY WADSWORTH LONGFELLOW
"The Wreck of the Hesperus"

To thine own self be true,
And it must follow, as night the day,
Thou canst not then be false to any man.
—WILLIAM SHAKESPEARE
Hamlet

CHAPTER 1

Shortly before 1:30 A.M. on Monday, November 26, 2001, Cantonment, Florida, resident Ed Harris awoke from a sound sleep to a "popping" noise that was coming from a nearby house. After rubbing the sleep from his eyes, Harris looked out his window and saw his neighbor's house on fire. He immediately called the fire department and reported what he was seeing, and informed the dispatcher that he believed that the occupant of the house, Terry Lee King, was at home. He knew, he said, because he could see King's car, a blue 1999 Dodge Shadow, parked in the driveway.

It was a typically sticky night at 66 degrees and nearly triple digit humidity in this small panhandle community, 18 miles northwest of Pensacola, as the Escambia County firefighters arrived at the King residence, located at 1104 Muscogee Road. They discovered that the home was secured, with the doors locked from the inside. Wasting no time, fireman Marcus Williamson entered the house after kicking in the front door, while another door on the east side of the house was kicked in by fireman David Jordan.

Several other firefighters followed Williamson and Jordan, trampling everything underfoot as they dragged their water hoses and equipment along with them.

While the fire was being extinguished, other firefighters went room-to-room searching for the house's inhabitants. Although it was only a few days after Thanksgiving, the fire investigators found a box of Christmas decorations as they entered another room that had been painted green. With Christmas less than a month away, it was obvious that the occupants were getting ready to decorate their home.

It wasn't until they closely examined the room, however, located at the east end of the house, that they found anyone. There was a man sitting in a chair with his legs propped up on a sofa. The man was wearing shoes, pants and a camouflage jacket, and he had a coffee cup sitting beside his right leg between his leg and the chair. There was a *Lion King* pillow on the couch next to the man, indicating that a child or children might reside in the home with him, and there was a blanket on the couch as well. There was a plate of food on the other side of the room, placed next to a chair. Many at the scene wondered why it had not been eaten.

When they first saw the man, firefighters thought that he had been overcome by smoke and flames. However, upon closer examination the firefighters observed that he had obvious injuries to his head, and they saw that there was considerable blood spatter on the walls around him.

After an examination at the scene that included a check for vital signs, the man tentatively identified as Terry King was pronounced dead at 2:02 A.M. by

Susie Whitfield of the Escambia County Emergency Medical Services, a group of specially trained medical professionals who respond to high-risk incidents such as the one being investigated. ECEMS provides tactical medical support to the sheriff's office and other agencies. Sadly, in this case all they could do was to establish that the victim was indeed dead and that no life-saving efforts were needed. It was a near certainty that he had not died as a result of the fire. It had suddenly become obvious that a homicide had been committed there, and that a fire likely had been started to conceal the crime. The firefighters cleared the house and notified the Escambia County Sheriff's Office and the Florida State Fire Marshal's Office.

After making a cursory examination of the home's interior, the firemen could see that the blaze had begun towards the rear of the house, on the dwelling's west side, inside what appeared to be the master bedroom. Williamson and Jordan, accompanied by other fire department investigators and sheriff's deputies, noted that a can of accelerant of an unknown type was in the doorway of the master bedroom. The can had been crushed, apparently by the rush of firefighters as they attempted to extinguish the flames.

Jim Sanders, battalion chief for the Escambia County Fire Rescue, told a group of reporters that had shown up outside the home that it had taken firefighters about thirty minutes to get the blaze under control. Much of the house, however, had been gutted by the fire, with estimated damage at approximately $40,000. It was a total loss, according to Sanders. He told the news media that it had not taken long for the firefighters to realize that the dead man, identified as

Terry Lee King, 40, had not succumbed to death because of the fire.

"The way he was found and the condition he was in led us to believe that there was some extenuating circumstances," Sanders said. "He was clear on the other side of the house [from where the blaze had started]."

Among the Escambia County investigations and crime-scene personnel to arrive were investigators Carol Turner and Glenn Gowitzke, who took control of the scene. Identification officers Ricky Barefield and Jan Johnson were also present. While Turner, Gowitzke, Barefield and Johnson busied themselves with the preliminary details, Detective John Sanderson was called at home shortly after 3 A.M. and informed that a probable homicide had been committed in his jurisdiction and that he had caught the assignment. In the meantime, Gowitzke, along with Kevin Fiedor of the State Fire Marshal's Office, determined that they were dealing with a case of homicide and arson.

It was foggy when Sanderson arrived at the Muscogee Road residence at 5:20 A.M., an hour before sunrise. Sanderson, a lanky middle-aged man of 46 with reddish-gray hair, was a seasoned professional. He began taking notes, both written and mental, immediately upon his arrival. He saw the blue Dodge Shadow, Florida license plate identification DP2-RF, in the driveway, and confirmed that it was registered to Terry King.

The fire investigators explained to Sanderson how they had initially thought that King had been overcome by smoke and flames, but that upon closer examination they had found the head wounds and the blood spatter on the walls. When Sanderson looked closely at the scene himself he thought that he detected traces of brain tissue mixed in with the blood spatter. One look at King's obviously battered skull served to back up the detective's opinion about brain matter, but the official determination would be made after the scene had been gone over by evidence technicians and analyzed at the crime lab. All that Sanderson knew at this point was that someone had certainly worked this poor bastard over in a most violent manner. Based on the obvious lack of a struggle, King likely never even saw the attack coming. Even the coffee cup was still sitting by his leg, where he might have placed it himself.

While Sanderson and the fire investigators remained inside the house, investigator Carol Turner began canvassing the neighborhood asking questions of various neighbors in the hope that someone might be able to shed some light on why anyone would want to murder Terry King.

"He stayed pretty much to himself," said neighbor Gladys Adams. "I would see him working out in the yard."

Adams told Turner that King had moved into the neighborhood a few months earlier, during the summer of 2001, and during those first few months she only saw one other person who appeared to live there, a young boy who looked like he might be barely a teenager.

"[That was] up until about two or three weeks ago," she said, "then we noticed another child over there. There were two boys getting off the bus with our granddaughter."

Other neighbors confirmed that King had moved

into the house on Muscogee Road during the summer, but no one knew them and no one had bothered to try to get acquainted with the family. Turner told Sanderson what little she had learned and wrote up an official report of her interviews with the neighbors.

So where were the boys? Sanderson wondered. Had they been kidnapped by the intruder who had killed their father? Or were they staying with friends or relatives?

Further investigation soon revealed that the two boys, Alex King, 12, and Derek King, 13, had been reported missing by their father a few days earlier. However, as the day wore on, Sanderson learned that the boys had been seen with their father only hours earlier, Sunday afternoon, November 25, outside in the yard. According to what Sanderson learned, Terry King had called the *Pensacola News Journal* on Thanksgiving Day and had complained that his sons had been missing from their home since November 16, the Friday before Thanksgiving, and that he was not satisfied that the local law enforcement agencies, particularly the Escambia County Sheriff's Department, were doing enough to find them. He told a reporter that the last time he had seen Alex and Derek was when he dropped them off at Ransom Middle School that morning. He stated that he did not think that they had run away from home because they had not taken anything with them. Instead, he said that he believed someone had kidnapped them. Although King had sounded upset when he spoke with the reporter, he could not name anyone he believed might have taken the boys. He did state that he did not have legal custody of Alex and Derek because he and the boys' mother had never been married to each other, and she now resided in Kentucky.

CHAPTER 2

At approximately 6:50 A.M., Detective John Sanderson met with James Walker, Sr., step-grandfather to Alex and Derek, who had shown up at the scene after being informed of the tragedy. Walker told Sanderson that he had received a telephone call the previous evening at 9 P.M., nearly five hours prior to the report of the fire. The call, he said, had been from Ricky Chavis, 40, a family friend, who informed him that Alex and Derek were at home with their father after having been missing for nearly a week. Walker explained to Sanderson that Chavis had told him about a green room that Terry King had used for "counseling" the boys, where he would just stare at them for hours. The room, Walker said, had been referred to by Chavis as the "therapy room." Chavis told Walker that King had said he was going to have a long "therapy" session with the boys that evening. Walker told Sanderson that it had been Chavis who had informed him, after the fire, that Terry King was dead.

Later, during the early morning hours of November 26, after the fire had been extinguished, Chavis had also informed Walker about the house fire as well as the fact that Alex and Derek were missing again. Chavis apparently told Walker that he had heard the fire call go out at the residence and that he had shown up there. It appeared that Chavis was privy to the information about the house fire as well as King's death at about the same time, or perhaps even just prior to it that the cops became privy to the information. Walker said that Chavis told him that Terry King was the only person at home at the time the fire was extinguished. Apparently Chavis told Walker that firemen working at the scene whom he knew had allowed him inside the house, and that King was too badly burned to identify. Chavis said, however, that he recognized King by the pants he was wearing, which were the same pair Chavis had seen him in a day earlier.

As Sanderson continued his interview, Walker told him that Chavis had speculated that King's death might turn out to be a criminal case. If it did, Chavis allegedly said he would go to court and testify that Alex and Derek had suffered some kind of abuse. Chavis also claimed that the two boys had taken all of the knives inside the house with them the last time they'd run away from home. Although Walker stated that he and his wife had not spent much time with Alex and Derek, they understood that things had not always been good for the boys. Walker said that to his knowledge, Terry King did not have alcohol or drug problems.

Later that morning Sanderson contacted Terry King's mother, Joyce Tracy, at her apartment in nearby Pensacola. As gently as he could, he delivered the bad news: Her son had been found dead at his

home and no one seemed to know what had become
of Alex and Derek. Tearfully, she told the detective
that her son did not have many guests, and that his
closest friend was Rick Chavis. As they talked, Ms.
Tracy explained that she and her family, including
Terry, had spent a great deal of time searching for
the two boys after they ran away from home on the
16th. She told Sanderson that Alex had called Rick
Chavis on the previous day to ask him for a ride. She
said that Chavis apparently found Alex hiding behind
the Tom Thumb store located at Spencer Field Road
and Highway 90 in nearby Milton, Florida. Alex was
then reunited with his father and Derek.

According to Tracy's statement, she had been
planning to speak to her son that very morning about
going with him to Ransom Middle School so that he
could introduce her to school officials and teachers
and inform them that she would be picking up Alex
and Derek from school on a regular basis. She also
explained that the boys had been in foster care for
several years and that they had resided at a place for
foster children called Heritage House until it closed
down. After Heritage House closed, Alex lived with
his father, but Derek had remained with a foster family for seven years and only recently reunited with
his father and brother. Derek, she said, had been staying with Frank Lay, a school principal, and his wife,
Nancy, in Pace. However, the Lays eventually returned Derek to his father because they began having
difficulty with him.

Ms. Tracy explained that Alex and Derek had run
away because they said that they did not have enough
freedom at home. They began hanging out with
friends in the vicinity of the Brentwood subdivision

near East Spencer Field Road, camping outdoors near a pond. She, too, said that she had been aware that the boys had taken a lot of knives with them when they had initially run away from home.

"Do you recall what the boys were wearing the last time you saw them?" Sanderson asked.

Ms. Tracy explained that when she last saw the boys, Derek was wearing black denim pants, a dark shirt and white tennis shoes. Alex was wearing faded denim pants, and tennis shoes without socks. She thought that Alex was wearing a dark jacket with a hood. He liked to wear jackets, she said. Derek, according to Ms. Tracy's statement, had told his father that he was using drugs, drinking alcohol and smoking tobacco.

Sanderson could only wonder where Alex and Derek were now, and what they were doing. Finding them as quickly as possible was a priority, but he didn't have a lot to go on yet.

Tracy explained that she spoke with her son nearly every day, and that his untimely death had been a total shock to the family and everyone who knew him.

"He was a very giving person," Tracy said. "He'd give you the shirt off his back without expecting anything in return." She had lived with her son and Alex for about a year, she added, during the time that Derek was still living in the foster home.

As the investigators worked throughout the day and into the evening hours trying to piece together what had actually occurred at the King residence early that morning, they simultaneously tried to locate the boys. Except for a neighbor who had seen them outside in the yard with their father on the af-

ternoon of November 25, the detectives had been unable so far to find anyone else who had seen them
with Terry after they had been reunited with him after
having run away from home the week before. That
leg of the investigation seemed to stop there.

"We're trying to do both things at once," Detective
Sanderson said to reporters in response to questions
about their handling of the death investigation and
the search for the two children. "These are twelve-
and thirteen-year-old kids, and we're very concerned
about their safety right now."

After speaking with an official with the Escambia
County School District, Sanderson learned that King
had taken his sons out of Ransom Middle School on
Monday, November 12. It was at that time that the
boys apparently informed their teachers that they
were moving to Kentucky. Then, a little more than a
week later, on Wednesday, November 21, King re-
enrolled Alex and Derek at Ransom Middle School,
apparently without explanation. According to what a
school district official told Sanderson, the two boys
were not with their father when he came into the
school to re-enroll them. Apparently no one at the
school had seen them since they were taken out
of school on November 12.

So where could they be? Sanderson wondered.

While Sanderson remained busy conducting interviews throughout the afternoon and into the evening
hours, Detective Carol Turner drove to Rick Chavis's
residence, a trailer home on Palm Court that Chavis
had shared with his brother, Mike, for several years.
After speaking briefly about the events of the past
day, Chavis agreed to accompany Turner to the sheriff's office for an interview with her and other detec-

tives. The interview was already under way by the time Sanderson arrived at 10:45 P.M.

Chavis told Sanderson and the other detectives who were present that he, Terry King and King's mother, Joyce Tracy, had spent much of the day in Santa Rosa County searching for Alex. Derek apparently had returned home the previous day. Chavis's account of the search for Alex was very similar to that of Ms. Tracy: Chavis received a telephone call from Alex, who had asked him to pick him up behind the Tom Thumb store and take him home. He then turned Alex over to Joyce Tracy, and a short time later Terry and Derek arrived. Upon their arrival, according to Chavis, Alex did not appear to want to go with his father and brother. Chavis suggested that he walk Alex to a nearby McDonald's and get him something to eat, to which Terry apparently agreed. Chavis claimed that he spoke to both Alex and Derek during that time frame, and both boys had indicated to him that they were concerned about going home with their father. During Chavis's account of the previous day's events he repeatedly told Sanderson that he needed to contact Escambia County Deputy Reggie Jernigan because Jernigan was aware of everything that was occurring between Terry King and his kids.

When asked to clarify what he meant, Chavis stated that Terry had been abusing the boys, mostly in a psychological manner. Chavis indicated that he had had words with Terry about the alleged abuse, particularly the manner in which he stared or looked at the boys, especially Alex, for long periods of time. Chavis said that he left Alex with Terry at approximately 2 P.M. on November 25, 2001.

As the interview continued into the night, Chavis told Sanderson how he had contacted James Walker, Sr., the boys' step-grandfather, at approximately 8:30 P.M. on November 25 to inform him that the boys were back at home with their father. He claimed that Terry and the boys were supposed to have come to his house that evening, but they never showed up. Although Walker said that Chavis claimed to have entered King's house after hearing of the fire over his scanner, Chavis stated that he had not gone into the house. He stated that he attempted to gain entry but was not allowed to go inside. Sanderson recalled how Walker had told him that Chavis, in his telephone call to Walker, claimed to have seen Terry's body, too badly burned to identify, but he had been able to recognize him by the pants that Terry was wearing.

Why such a discrepancy? Sanderson wondered.

Chavis said that Terry told him the boys had taken a lot of knives with them when they ran away from home, and that Derek had become very cold toward his father. Chavis also stated, without going into detail, that his friend had been withdrawing from him lately, having less and less to do with him. Chavis commented that if Terry's death turned out to be a homicide, the boys must have had something to do with it.

Why was Chavis suddenly suggesting that Alex and Derek had something to do with their father's death? Sanderson wondered. Did Chavis know more than he was saying? Or were there other reasons? His interest in Chavis's statements growing stronger, Sanderson urged Chavis to continue.

Chavis explained that Alex once told him that weekends at the King residence were sometimes used for "therapy" sessions during which the boys could not speak—they could only stare at each other. Although Chavis said that he had never witnessed any physical abuse between Terry and the boys, he claimed that Alex once told him that his dad had hit him. Chavis said that Alex did not like his dad, and that he had heard Derek make a recent statement, within two weeks of Terry's slaying, that he wished his dad was dead. Chavis said that Derek made his remark in Chavis's front yard prior to running away from home. Chavis also said that Alex had stated a couple of months earlier that he wished someone would kill his father.

According to Chavis's statement, it appeared as if Terry had been strict with Alex and Derek. Chavis cited as an example that, when the boys would get home from school, they were required to go inside the house, lock the doors and not communicate with anyone until Terry picked them up and took them to work with him at Pace Printing. Terry did not have a telephone in the house, according to Chavis, and two-way radios were used for communications between them. As for the boys having problems at school, Chavis said he had heard that kids at Ransom Middle School frequently picked on Derek. The boys had only attended Ransom for approximately three months. Although Derek had claimed to be taking drugs, using alcohol and smoking cigarettes, Chavis stated that Terry King did not drink.

When asked about any friends or enemies that Terry might have had, Chavis responded that Terry did not have any other friends, and that Chavis did not know of any problems he might have had with others. Chavis went on to say that he and Terry were not very close, but that he had tried to be Terry's friend. He said that he had met Terry through a relative of Derek and Alex's mother, Janet French. He had not spent much time with Alex and Derek recently because he had gotten too close to them, Chavis said. It seemed at times that Terry did not want the boys to spend too much time with him.

When asked where he thought the boys might be now, Chavis said that it was possible that they had gone back to the Pace area. Chavis said that the last time he saw the boys, he believed that Derek was wearing blue shorts with white trim and a blue shirt, and that Alex was wearing jeans and a white tee shirt, as well as a black jacket. The last time he saw Terry King, Chavis said that he was wearing a white tee shirt, blue jeans and a camouflage cap.

As Sanderson concluded the interview, he asked Chavis if he could go to his residence to see if the boys had left any messages on his answering machine. Chavis agreed, and when they listened to the tape, there was a message from Alex instructing Chavis to tell his father that he and his brother were not coming home. It was not clear what time the call had come in—it may have been placed prior to their father's death. At any rate, Sanderson recorded it and took the copy with him. As Sanderson left Chavis's home, Chavis told him that he would do everything he could to help find the boys.

The various accounts of the events that led up to Terry King's death seemed convoluted and confusing, and did little at this point to direct the cops toward what might have happened to Alex and Derek after their father's slaying.

The confusion had only begun.

CHAPTER 3

At one point early in the investigation on November 27, Detectives John Sanderson and Terry Kilgore paid a visit to Frank Lay, the principal of Pace High School, on Norris Road in Pace. They hoped that Lay could offer some background information on Alex and Derek that might help locate the boys. Lay, a man of medium height and weight, approaching middle age but still possessing a youthful persona, invited the detectives into his office and appeared willing to discuss his relationship with the boys and what he knew about the King family.

Lay told the detectives that several years earlier the Kings' children were left at the Heritage Home by their parents. When it closed down, Derek lived with Lay and his wife, Nancy, for approximately seven years. During that time they had very little contact with Terry King. However, Derek told them that his father would lock him inside a closet and engage in "mind games" with him. At one point Derek's grades began to slip, and it got to the point where he stopped studying altogether. Lay warned him that he needed to "straighten up" and do what was expected of a child his age, particularly with regard to his schoolwork, or he would not be able to continue living with the Lays. Finally, in early October 2001, the Lays decided that Derek had become too hard to handle and returned him to his father. About a month after Derek returned home, Lay said that he received a call that Derek had run away.

On Sunday night, November 25, 2001, only hours prior to Terry King's slaying, the Lays received a telephone call and were informed that Derek was at a neighbor's home. However, when they went to pick him up, he attempted to run away from them. When they finally caught him, Derek was visibly upset and told the Lays that he could not return home because "dad uses mind games" and other things of that type. According to Lay's statement, Derek told him that he had been staying with Rick Chavis. Chavis, according to what Derek told Lay, had put Derek and Alex up at his trailer after they had run away from home.

Lay related another conversation that he'd had with Derek shortly after the boy had been located on November 25. During that conversation, Derek told Lay that his brother Alex hated their father and had said that he wanted to kill him. Derek, according to Lay, had described Terry King as a "control freak" who would not let them go anywhere and kept them locked inside the house. Derek also told Lay that their father had subjected him and Alex to mental abuse. According to Lay, Derek had insisted that Chavis protected the boys from their father. When Terry would go to Chavis's home looking for them, Alex and Derek would hide from him. Derek also told Lay that the fact that they would even stay at

Chavis's home was something that they had planned in advance with Chavis. Lay said Derek told him that he was going to call Rick and ask for a ride home on November 25.

A short time later Sanderson and Kilgore interviewed Rebecca Hubbard, a teenage girl who went to Pace High School. Hubbard told the detectives that she had been acquainted with Derek King for only a couple of months and that she had last seen him on November 25, when Derek came to her house and informed her that he had been kicked out of the Lays' house. He also told her that he was staying with Rick Chavis and that Chavis was to meet him at the Tom Thumb store. Hubbard told the cops that on that same Sunday a man whom she described as fitting Chavis's description came to her home at approximately 7:30 P.M. and told her that he had dropped Derek off nearby and was looking for him. Derek apparently had shown up at Hubbard's house around 4 P.M. that same day, but had stayed only thirty minutes or so. She told Sanderson that Derek had called a man named Rick from her house. She also told Sanderson that Derek had talked about using drugs often, and she'd noticed that he had cigarettes on him. She said that Derek had indicated to her that his dad was a "control freak" and that he didn't want to go back home to live with him.

That same day Sanderson and Kilgore interviewed Rick Chavis again at the sheriff's office. During the questioning, Chavis told the detectives that Alex and Derek had run away from home on or about November 9, 2001, and that Terry King had wanted to cancel the missing persons report. Rick said that he dialed the phone for Terry and that Terry cancelled the report on his sons. It was not clear from Chavis's statement why Terry had done this. Since Chavis didn't know or would not say, the investigators wondered if Chavis had played a role in getting Terry to cancel. Later in the week Terry called back and reinstated the report since the boys had not returned home. Afterward Chavis said that he received a telephone call from Alex, who purportedly told Chavis that he was okay. Then, on Sunday, November 25, Chavis said that he received a phone call from Alex asking him to come and pick him up. Chavis said that he went to the Tom Thumb on Spencer Field Road looked around and found Alex hiding behind the store. Derek, meanwhile, had returned home the day before, according to Chavis, who said that he had received a phone call from Terry King to that effect. Although Alex had been briefly reunited with his father, Chavis said that he had asked Terry for permission to take Alex to get something to eat at a nearby McDonald's, which he did. Chavis said that Terry, Derek and Alex were supposed to have come by his home later that same evening.

At one point Chavis reiterated what he had been telling others regarding the events surrounding Terry King's death, including the fact that he had heard the fire call go out at King's residence and that he had personally gone there. He also told the detectives that the last time he had seen Derek, prior to seeing him on November 25, had been before November 9, 2001. He also recalled how both Alex and Derek had come by his home on Halloween night, and his recollection led the detectives through details of his friendship with Terry.

Chavis recollected how he and Terry King had

been friends for a long time, but that they'd had a falling out a few years ago. A week after their disagreement, Terry had apologized to him. Chavis didn't go into detail about what had caused the two men to quarrel but said that their relationship had been somewhat distant until recently. According to Chavis, he and Terry had been getting closer again lately. Terry had started coming over to Chavis's home again within the past year, and had asked if he could bring Alex along with him on his visits. Chavis had agreed that he could, and that was when he had first met Alex.

Chavis said that he soon realized that Alex was a good kid, but described Derek as having been "wild," a characterization that Terry had related to him on one occasion after getting Derek back from foster care. Chavis stated that Terry used to smoke pot, but that he had quit shortly after getting Derek back. Chavis, admitting that he, too, had smoked pot, said that he had last smoked it with Terry approximately one year earlier, and that he had smoked pot only twice in the past year. Chavis stated that Terry did not smoke pot with Alex and Derek, at least not that he was aware of, and that he had no knowledge of Terry ever supplying either of the boys with cigarettes, alcohol or drugs.

Chavis told the cops that when Alex and Derek were reunited with their father, there was much hard friction between them. Some of it stemmed from the so-called "therapy" sessions that were held in the green room. Chavis recounted one example that was related to him by Alex in which Alex, Derek and Terry would just stare at each other for long periods of time without speaking. Chavis also stated that

Terry had recently installed a dead-bolt lock on the front door of his home and to which he kept the keys. Chavis claimed that once in the recent past, Terry had threatened to do harm to James Walker, Sr., the boys' step-grandfather, because Walker apparently had been attempting to gain custody of one of the boys. At the time of the interview, Chavis told the cops that he did not know where the boys were hiding out or what might have become of them.

A short time later Sanderson received information that a man named Lewis Michael Tyson might have information potentially useful to the case. When Sanderson followed up early on the afternoon of November 27, he learned that Tyson had known Terry King for approximately eight years. Tyson explained that Terry, Derek and Alex had shown up at his home at approximately 10 P.M. on November 25, 2001, during which time they all talked. Tyson said that the boys had acted very strange during the visit, particularly because they were hugging Terry and playing around each other. They seemed to be happy, but Tyson claimed that the hugging they were doing was unusual and out of character for them.

He said that Alex had called his father by his first name that evening. Tyson claimed that he knew Alex very well, and knew that the only time the boy called his father by his first name was when he was angry with him. Tyson said that they had stayed at his house until 12:15 A.M. He said he was certain of the time because he had checked his watch as they were leaving. Just prior to their departure he said that he asked the boys where they had been when they ran away, and he said that they claimed to have been with a person by the name of "Jim." "Jim" had picked up the boys and they had been with him the entire week that they were gone. The boys had told Tyson that they liked "Jim" a lot, and described his residence as a large house with cameras on the outside and wire on top of his fence. They also stated that he had a good computer system. As Sanderson reflected on the information, he realized that the descriptions Alex and Derek had provided of "Jim's" home also applied to that of Rick Chavis.

CHAPTER 4

Later that same day, November 27, 2001, Sanderson drove to Ransom Middle School, which Alex and Derek attended. Upon his arrival, Sanderson spoke with Debbie Alltop, a school employee. After conversing generally about the boys, Alltop told Sanderson that Terry King had come into the office earlier in the year and had provided special instructions for having the boys picked up after school. According to Alltop, Terry had given special "checkout" orders for a man who resided on Palm Court to collect the boys each day. From the description that she provided, Sanderson believed the man to be Rick Chavis.

According to Alltop, two weeks earlier the man Sanderson believed to be Chavis had come into the school and spoken with her. During that conversation the man was adamant that Terry wanted him to pick up Alex and Derek. During that same visit, the man paid for a cookbook that the school was selling and that he was supposed to have given to Terry, along with a message that Alltop gave him about a parent–teacher conference. The man claimed that Terry did not want the boys staying alone after school and wanted them to go home with him.

However, Terry showed up at the school approximately two days later and picked up the boys. When Alltop informed him about the man, Terry became very angry and stated that that man was never to pick the boys up again. At that time Alltop learned that Terry had never received the cookbook from the man, nor had he been given the message about the parent–teacher conference. Terry had asked Alltop to pull all the files that referenced the man picking up his sons. Sanderson found paperwork with the subject's name on it—it was Rick Chavis.

Sanderson next spoke with Deputy Wayne Ladieu, Ransom Middle School's resource officer. He stated that on November 21, the Wednesday before the fire, Terry had come into the school asking to see the principal as well as Officer Ladieu. After previously having withdrawn Alex and Derek from the school on November 19, supposedly to take them to live in Kentucky, Terry now wanted to re-enroll them at Ransom because their plans had fallen through. At that time Terry also told the principal and the officer that both boys were missing.

Hopeful that he could obtain additional information regarding the events of the evening of November 25, Sanderson again contacted Lewis Michael Tyson at his home on November 27th. During that second interview, Tyson told Sanderson that Terry King had appeared very nervous the evening he and the boys visited. Tyson also said that Terry had related to him that he did not trust Derek. Tyson said that Terry then told him that he had read diaries and other things that caused him to feel that way, and that the diaries,

along with Rick Chavis's digital camera and some
photos were inside the trunk of his car. Terry apparently did not reveal the nature of the photos or what
they depicted.

Sanderson took note. This was an interesting development. Tyson told him that Terry said he was
going to sleep on the couch when he got home that
evening. Terry further said, according to Tyson, that
he was going to place Alex in his bedroom and Derek
in the other bedroom. He was going to sleep on the
couch because of his distrust of the two boys, and
was going to deadbolt the other doors in the house.
While Tyson and King were talking that evening, the
two boys were in Tyson's back yard on a swing, in
some kind of a deep discussion. Tyson said that he
and Terry had jokingly stated something to the effect
of, "They look like they're plotting something."

As Sanderson began to put background information together about Terry King, he learned that he
was a high-school dropout who had worked sporad-
ically at local printing plants, most recently in nearby
Pace. He had fathered Alex and Derek with a woman
named Janet Lyttle, but never married her. At one
point she had twins with another man, and approximately eight years earlier, she had left Terry, Alex
and Derek. She worked for a short time as a nightclub
dancer, then changed her name to Kelly Marino, got
married and moved to Kentucky. Terry King, in the
meantime, struggled to raise Alex and Derek, along
with Janet's twins, usually at little more than $7 per
hour. He often worked nights. Unable to make ends
meet, Terry eventually gave up the twins by putting
them up for adoption, and he sent Alex and Derek to
live in a number of foster homes, and with friends

and relatives. By the time he was able to bring Alex and Derek back home, he had managed to obtain a house for all of them to live in together.

"Terry had reached a goal he'd been trying a long time to attain, that is, having a house for him and the boys," Wilbur King said. Wilbur said that he had not seen his son often recently because of conflicts in their job schedules—Terry's night shift at the printing plant and Wilbur's day job as a meat cutter at one of the local Food World stores—and in part because of Wilbur's duties as an ordained minister.

"He was quiet," Wilbur said. "But he was a hard-working person, and he worked hard raising those boys. He had just bought that house this summer, and we just sold him a car. He was real proud of that car. . . . This has been hell. It's just been shock. Total shock."

While Sanderson and Kilgore handled one aspect of the investigation, other investigators continued to canvass King's neighborhood in search of clues and additional background on King and his two boys. It was a quiet neighborhood in which the residents were accustomed to leaving their garages, as well as their homes, unlocked.

"Not anymore," said one neighbor, Kathryn Bryan, 66. "This horrifies me. I just called Gulf Power to come put some lights in the back."

"I saw the boy working in the yard with his dad all the time," Bryan continued. She said that that was where Terry spent most of his spare time, as did Alex, because Terry liked gardening. "I was concerned about the boy because I never saw him playing. He never had a ball or anything. He just followed his daddy around."

Another neighbor, Ted Johnson, 30, echoed what Bryan had said. "My doors get locked now," Johnson declared. "That's the weird thing. Nothing ever happens in Cantonment, hardly. For that to happen out here, right across the street at that time of night, it's extremely shocking."

Yet another neighbor, Gladys Hobbs, who lived across the street from King, told investigators that Terry kept to himself. Like Bryan, Hobbs said that the only time they saw him was when he was working in the yard. "I don't know them at all," Hobbs said. "But it's terrible. It's awful. We keep our doors locked now. It just reminds us that things like that can happen real near you."

A short time later, as Sanderson prepared to check on the status of the search for Alex and Derek, he was contacted by Lt. Tracy Yuhasz, who told him the search was over. According to what Yuhasz reported, Rick Chavis and Deputy Reggie Jernigan were on their way to the sheriff's office with the two boys as they spoke. They arrived at the Escambia County Sheriff's Office shortly after 3 P.M. Sanderson and Kilgore each spoke briefly with Rick when he brought the boys in. Chavis told the detectives that a girl, whom he said he did not know, had called him from a cell phone requesting that he pick them up. Could it have been Rebecca Hubbard who had called? Sanderson and Kilgore wondered. He said he found them in neighboring Santa Rosa County. Chavis claimed that the boys told him shortly after he picked them up that Derek had beaten his father with a baseball bat after Terry had thrown Alex across a table and to the floor in the so-called "green room."

News that the boys had been found traveled quickly throughout the community, and it was only a matter of minutes before the media began probing.

"Technically, they're not under arrest," Chief Deputy Larry Smith told eager reporters. "They are in our safekeeping until we decide the appropriate place for them. At this particular time, we cannot adequately say if they're witnesses or suspects. Obviously, as far as we know, they were the last people to see him [King] alive. . . . So now our thing is—what do they know that we don't?"

According to Smith, after the boys had been questioned, they would likely spend the night in juvenile detention, regardless of whether Sanderson and Kilgore viewed them as witnesses or suspects. The state attorney's office stepped quickly into the picture to make certain that all laws and procedures regarding the interrogation of children were followed.

Family members were, of course, very relieved to learn that the boys had been found and were safe. However, concern now centered on whether they had anything to do with their father's death. Most family members said they did not believe that the two boys were capable of committing acts of violence.

"I don't think there's any way they could even think about doing that," Joyce Tracy, Terry's mother and the boys' grandmother, said. "They were loving children, and they couldn't have done that."

Tracy told investigators that she had spoken with her son nearly every day, and that she had lived with him and Alex for nearly a year while her apartment was being remodeled. Derek, she said, was not living with them at that time.

"At this point, it's just a relief that those boys are

safe," Tracy stated. She said that simply because the children ran away from home did not mean that they were guilty of, or capable of committing, such a violent crime. "Going away from home and camping out is one thing," Tracy said. "But doing something violent is quite another thing altogether. Alex is quiet, but he's a loving child. When Derek came back, he was glad to be home. They were both so happy to be with each other."

Terry King's uncle, Woody King, also expressed relief that the boys had been found safe. However, he said that he had not seen Terry for several months.

"He was a good guy," Woody King said. "Never heard a cross word out of him or about him. I just pray that they clear up whatever happened and whoever did this so his mom and dad can rest a little easier. It's not easy for one to lose your young'un."

Before going in to interview the boys, Sanderson decided to review the series of events as they had unfolded so that he would be able to more easily detect any inconsistencies in anything that either of the boys might say. He knew, for instance, that Terry King had called the sheriff's department on November 16, 2001, and had reported that Alex and Derek were missing. He had dropped them off at school that morning, and discovered that they were missing later in the day. At that time he told deputies that he did not believe that the boys had run away from home, but that he feared they had been taken by someone, and that when he came home that day he had found only one book bag, and a Game Boy was missing. However, none of the boys' clothes were gone.

The next day, November 17, according to one of the follow-up reports, Terry had received a telephone call from Derek, who told him that he and Alex knew that he was looking for them. However, he told his father that they were not coming home again. Two days later, Terry went to the school and withdrew them, claiming that they were going to Kentucky. The following day he called the sheriff's office again and reported that his boys were still missing. The next day Terry went back to Ransom and told school officials that he wanted to re-enroll his boys even though they were still missing. On November 22, Terry called the local newspaper, the *Pensacola News Journal*, and complained that although he had reported his sons missing to the sheriff's department, local law enforcement officials were not doing anything to help find them. Two days later, November 24, Derek was found and returned to his father by Escambia County Deputy Sheriff Thomas Mohan.

During the ride home Derek asked Mohan how to file an abuse claim against his father. When asked why he wanted to file such a claim, Derek told Mohan that his father did not allow him to watch much television and that he was picky about who he allowed Derek, as well as Alex, to associate with. Mohan told Derek that it sounded as if, to him, Terry King was a good father.

The next day, Alex was returned to his father after calling Rick Chavis for a ride. The following day Terry King was dead.

CHAPTER 5

Shortly past 5 P.M. on November 27, Derek and Alex King were taken into separate interrogation rooms at the Escambia County Sheriff's Office. John Sanderson was present, as was investigator Terry Lee Kilgore.

The boys now realized that they were there because they were being investigated in connection with the slaying of their father, and each was to provide a recorded statement to the detectives. After speaking with Chavis, the detectives asked if either of them were thirsty or needed to go to the bathroom. Derek told them he was thirsty and they provided him with a Coke.

Prior to beginning the official interview, the detectives talked somewhat informally with the boys and by doing so, developed a good rapport with them. After a couple of hours of getting acquainted, the detectives decided to take taped statements from the boys. Derek King went first while Alex waited in another room for his turn.

"Okay, Derek, this is an official form of the Escambia County Sheriff's Office and part of an investigative procedure," Kilgore explained as he showed Derek the form that the boy had signed upon being arrested. "It must be completed by all officers of the Escambia County Sheriff's Office. Before we ask you any questions, you must understand your rights. You have the right to remain silent. Anything you say can be used as evidence against you in court. You have the right to have a lawyer present while being questioned. If you cannot afford to hire a lawyer, a lawyer will be appointed for you without cost before questioning. If you wish to answer questions now without a lawyer present, you will still have the right to stop answering questions at any time. The waiver is, 'I have read this statement of my rights shown above and I understand what my rights are. No promises or threats have been made to me and no pressure of any kind has been used against me.' Derek, is that your signature that appears at the bottom of the page?"

"Yes, sir," Derek responded somewhat nervously as he examined the Miranda form.

"How old are you?" Kilgore asked.

"Thirteen," Derek responded. The paperwork showed that his date of birth was May 4, 1988, and listed his Social Security number as well.

"And what grade are you in at school?" the detective asked.

"Eighth," responded the child.

"Do you know how to read and write?"

"Yes, sir."

"Do you know the difference between right and wrong?"

"Yes, sir."

"We've been told—and we talked earlier before

the tape came on—that you have a very high IQ. Is
that correct?"

"Yes, sir."

"Recently you possibly should be or have been in
the gifted program at school?"

"Yes, sir."

"So you understand what's going on?"

"Yes, sir."

Kilgore seemed satisfied that he had established
that Derek knew right from wrong, understood his
rights and that he was of above-average intelligence
for his age.

"What we'd like to do is start and talk about what
happened at your house over on Muscogee Road.
Now, that would have been late Sunday night or early
Monday morning, and that would have been either
the twenty-fifth, Sunday, and the twenty-sixth, early
Monday morning . . . What we'd like for you to do
is just start, and you can say anything you want to
on tape, start from the beginning and let us know
what happened. Okay?"

"Okay."

"All right, go ahead," Kilgore urged.

"I caught my dad throwing my brother around, my
twelve-year-old brother, and . . ."

"If you would, start a little bit ahead of that," Sanderson interjected. "Just go back a little bit further
when we were talking about when you were . . . uh,
at this guy's house and where y'all went from there.
If you don't mind. Okay?"

"Okay. We were sitting on the swing and I told
Alex . . . if it gets real serious that I would get physical with Dad, and so . . ."

"Whose house were y'all at?" Sanderson interrupted again.

"Mike [Tyson's]."

"Mike. Do you know Mike very well or—Where do you know him from?" Sanderson probed.

"The flea market."

"Do you know what, about what time it was?" Sanderson asked. "Did anybody ask Mike what time it was, or did Mike say anything about what time it was before y'all left?"

"I saw his watch. I saw the time on his watch when his hands were crossed . . . Twelve midnight."

"How long had you been over at Mike's house?" Kilgore asked.

"I don't remember . . . I don't remember how long it was."

Approximately five minutes into the interrogation, Deputy Reggie Jernigan, whom the boys had met before, entered the room at Derek's request. He did not take part in the questioning.

"Where had you been earlier in the day? Do you remember that?" Kilgore asked.

"Flea market . . . We were at the flea market taking down signs."

"And the signs you were taking down—what were those?"

"Our, our missing pictures. Our flyers about us being missing."

"You're talking about earlier on, that you and your brother had run away from home?" Kilgore tried to clarify.

"Yes, sir."

"Do you remember what date that was that y'all run away?"

"No, sir."

"Okay. If I was to tell you that it was a Friday, on November 16th, does that sound about right?"

"That sounds about right."

"That would have been the week before Thanksgiving."

"Yes, sir."

"Does that sound about right to you?"

"Mm-hm. 'Cause we were gone Thanksgiving."

"So you're over at Mike's. You had been at the flea market earlier on in the day taking down signs . . . and you don't know how long you were over there . . ."

"No, sir."

"What was going on at Mike's house? What was happening?"

"What do you mean?"

"Well, I mean, what were you doing? What was your dad doing? What was Mike doing? What was Alex doing?"

"Well, Mike and my dad were talking. Most of the time it was privately . . . They were kind of being secretive about it, and then me and Alex were playing with his cats and his dog and just playing games and stuff. Having fun."

"Okay."

"And then we just sat down on the swing. I told Alex, 'If stuff gets serious, I will, I will defend you.' "

Sanderson eerily recalled Tyson's statement about how he and Terry had jokingly said to each other that the boys looked "like they're plotting something" as they sat on the swing at Tyson's house.

"What, what would make you say that? Why would you say that?"

" 'Cause Alex told me he, he was weak and he didn't have enough, he didn't have strength to fight him off . . . fight my father off."

"Did you feel like they might, something might happen?" Sanderson interjected. "I mean, that's what he's talking about, why y'all were having that conversation?"

"Why, because we, 'cause we were scared that something might, since we, he . . . That was the day he got both of us back. Um, I was, I was just afraid that once he got both of us back, he would get physical with both of us at, at, both of us at once."

"Is that because you ran away?" Kilgore asked.

"Yes."

"Well, let me ask you this. You got, you were brought back home on Saturday. And Saturday would have been the . . . Did your dad get physical with you then?"

"Hm-mm," he said, shaking his head no.

"Did he threaten you in any way?"

"No, sir . . . not like verbally."

"What do you mean?"

"Like he was, he was staring me down some."

"Let me ask you something about that," Sanderson said. "We were talking about it earlier. Has your dad ever hit y'all?"

"Not, not punched us or nothing, but he has thrown us around."

"Has he ever used any kind of, uh, weapons on you or anything?" Sanderson asked.

"No."

"Did he ever spank you with a belt or a switch or

. . . anything like that?" Sanderson probed.

"No."

"As far as pushing you around, how serious has that ever got?" Sanderson asked. "I mean, is it something that leaves physical marks on you or anything?"

"Barely . . . Um, I might trip over something and fall down."

"Now most of . . . what we've been talking about, we talked about some pushing around," Sanderson said. "Is that a frequent event, him pushing, or was it mostly something else that he would do?"

"Disciplinary action," Derek responded matter-of-factly.

"What kind of disciplinary action?" Sanderson asked. "Give me a for-instance."

"If we did something wrong like . . . we talk back to him."

"What would he do if you talked back?" Kilgore asked.

"Um, he would, he'd be like, he . . ."

"That's all right. Take your time."

"I don't want to waste the tape."

"Oh, don't worry about wasting the tape. We've got plenty of tape," Kilgore said.

"I forgot the question now."

"The question is, 'Give me a for-instance.' . . . For, like, a disciplinary action. You talk back . . . that's what we were talking about," Kilgore said. "What would he do to ya, if you talked back to him?"

"He'd be like, 'When I, when I say something, my answer's final,' and he'd be pushing us while he said that . . . And he said, 'When I, I mean, when I say yes, I mean yes, when I say no, I mean no, no questions about it . . . Do you understand?' He'd be pushing us around while he's saying that."

"Okay," Sanderson responded. "Let me ask you something on the same grounds, too. As far as, as far as food . . . Did he feed y'all good?"

"Yes, sir."

"Keep clothes on ya?" Sanderson asked.

"Yes, sir . . . He made us dress the way he felt about his way was right."

"Okay, so . . . you're at Mike's house, you're sitting on the bench. You talk about that . . ." Kilgore trailed off.

"Did y'all specifically say anything when you were sitting there?" Sanderson cut in.

"Not specifically," Derek replied. "I said, I said, 'I will, I will fight him off, and if it gets serious enough, I will kill him,'cause I, I know that you are not physically strong . . . you're not strong enough to fight [him] off.' And so, well, when we got home, 'cause he, he stared me down pretty good one time . . . while we were at Mike's house and, um, so when we got home, he dealt with Alex. Then I, I tried to get on his good side and cool him down, like hugging him. Stuff like that."

"Now you said [he] 'dealt with Alex,' " Kilgore stated. "What do you mean by that? What happened?"

"He shoved him around. He, he didn't really yell that much and . . ."

"Do you remember what he was saying?"

"No . . . And so he pushed him around, and he pushed him, and Alex fell on the table and started crying, and then I was, I was in, I was out of the room and I walked by and I caught him, I caught him as soon as, when he was pushing Alex, and then, uh, I was like . . ."

"Do you know what that was all about?" Sanderson asked.

"No. Not really . . . Well, actually, it was about running away . . . He was mad 'cause we ran away."

"But he didn't say nothing to you or anything about it at that time?" Sanderson asked.

"Mm-hm." Derek indicated that his father had not actually said anything to either Derek or his brother. He just assumed his father's anger was over them having run away from home.

"Okay," Sanderson interjected. "Having a conversation with Alex about [running away] when all this happened. Is that right or . . . ?"

"Yes . . . And . . . we, like, started playing and stuff with toys and I said, 'Don't worry about him. I'll, I'll deal with him.' So when he went to sleep, I got, I made sure he was asleep. I got the bat and I hit him over the head."

"Where was your dad at when, when you hit him?" Kilgore asked.

"In the green room."

"And the green room is just a part of the house? Is that correct?"

"Mm-hm. The last room, well, the only room on the, uh, right side of the house . . . right behind the concrete slab where the car's normally parked."

"Where was your dad asleep at?"

"On a, on a recliner . . . Feet propped on the couch. He had a coffee cup in his hand."

"And you're showing [demonstrating to] us a coffee cup and you've got it down almost on your inseam in your groin area. Is that correct?"

"Yes . . . And he either had his hand on the handle or he had it in, on the cup and I can't remember . . ."

"That's okay. So he's laying there and you've made sure he's asleep. . . . Tell me what happened then. . . . Where, where did you get the bat from?"

"Down the hall. A little ways down the hall."

"And we were talking about that earlier, and is that what you hit your father with?"

"Yes."

"Okay."

"Mainly the left side of his face and his, his head."

"Tell me about that now. And I know that that's painful, but, and we talked about it before, so tell me about it."

"I went in there," Derek said quietly. "I hit him once and then I heard him moan and then I was afraid that he might wake up and see us, so I just kept on hitting him. . . . Hit him somewhere around ten times."

"All the blows . . . What area?" Sanderson cut in.

"The face, the face, the left side of the face and forehead."

"You're saying the left, but you're patting the right side of your face," Kilgore pointed out.

"Well, it was right to me 'cause he was, he was laying down . . . Wait, no it wasn't, 'cause I was, I was hitting him. It was my right, his left."

"Okay. 'Cause you keep patting your right, and I just want to make sure because . . . the tape can't see what you're doing. . . . That's why we have to explain everything, so we make sure we get it all correct."

"Okay."

"So what happens after that? Where's Alex at when this is going on?"

"He was, he was right there beside me. . . . Watching me."

"Did he know you were gonna do it?"

"Mm-hm. Well, he, not, not . . . I, he knew what was up when I grabbed the bat."

"How do you know he knew what was up? Did you say something to Alex when you grabbed the bat?"

"It was too late to go play baseball," Derek simply responded.

"What was y'all's conversation between the time he shoved Alex and the time that your father fell asleep?" Sanderson asked. " 'Cause we know y'all had some kind of conversation."

"Well, Alex was just pretty . . . was really mad at him."

"What was y'all's conversation during that time when you were waiting for him to go to sleep?" Sanderson asked.

"Do you know about how long that was?" Kilgore asked.

"About five minutes or so. . . . Five or ten minutes. Somewhere around there."

"Okay."

"And, uh, so . . . he [Alex] was like, 'You'd better go ahead and do it if you're gonna do it.' Kill him . . . [Inaudible]"

"Is that what Alex said?"

"Mm-hm . . . that's what he meant. . . . I, I can't remember the exact words."

"He knew what you were gonna do . . ." Sanderson offered.

"Mm-hm."

"It was something y'all talked about. Is that correct or not?" Sanderson asked.

"Yeah, but we didn't do [it] in the specifics, like . . ."

"Not exactly how or anything," Sanderson cut in.

"Yeah. He just knew that something was gonna happen."

"So what happens after that?" Kilgore asked.

"I, I . . . I killed him. I run . . . I, I immediately . . . I can't, I can't stand to see his face 'cause I was scared. I, and I . . ."

"I'm sorry . . . and I don't mean to break in . . . but [what] was your initial feelings when you first did this?" Sanderson asked.

"Um, defense for Alex."

"No, I mean . . ." Sanderson said, trailing off.

"What do you mean?" Derek asked.

"I mean, how did you feel yourself when you first did this?" Sanderson clarified.

"I was mad that he, he did anything like that."

"Earlier you were asked that you know the difference between right and wrong . . . Okay. You do?" Sanderson asked.

"Mm-hm. [affirmative response] . . . But my anger just was so overwhelming that I just did what I thought was right."

"So after all this went down, then . . ." Sanderson probed.

"I threw the bat on the bed, lit the bed on fire because I was scared of the [evidence] and everything. Scared of getting caught and . . ."

"You lit the bed on fire. Did you light anything else on fire?" Kilgore asked.

"I tried to light the rug at the front door, but I don't think, I don't think, I don't think I did . . . because I picked the rug up and lit it. I, I lit the little frayed thing."

"You wet it?"

"I *lit* it."

"Oh, I'm sorry."

"Set it on fire."

"I'm sorry. I thought you said you *wet* it. Okay. Did you wet any of the house down?"

"No."

"So that was what bedroom? Where's that bedroom located?" Sanderson asked. "Where the bed was set on fire."

"The last bedroom on the . . . uh, left."

"And whose bedroom would that be?" Kilgore asked.

"My dad's."

"The bat was aluminum or wooden?" Sanderson asked.

"Aluminum."

"Now during that time, what was Alex doing?" Sanderson asked. "Think, think hard on exactly what he was doing as far as during that time."

"He was just watching me and following me right behind me."

"Did anybody at any time, uh, when you went to light the rug up at the front door and it wouldn't light . . ." Sanderson asked, unable to finish the question because he was cut off by Derek's response.

"Well, I don't know, but it just kind of blazed a little bit and then . . . I just threw it down and then Alex was like, uh, yeah, I forgot he [their dad] changed the [dead]bolt on the door so we couldn't get out, so we ran to the back, but first we ran into the room again, the green room, and we tried to get that door unlocked, but it didn't come unlocked. That little latch up top . . . the chain. It, it wouldn't come off, so we just went to the back door and then we went outside and we ran."

"You ran out what door?" Kilgore asked.

"The back door. The farthest one on the right of the house."

"When you're facing the house, on the right side," Kilgore suggested. "Okay. And where'd y'all run to?"

"We just ran to . . . Well, I don't know . . . I was just leading the way. We ran to a highway. We got somebody . . . a man to, um, to pick us up and take us to Pace . . ."

"Do you remember what he looked like?"

"No. I was too shook up about what happened to notice anything."

"You didn't know his name?" Sanderson asked.

"Hm-mm." [Negative response]

"Did he take you all the way over to Pace?"

"Yeah."

"Where did he drop you off at? Where'd you have him drop you off?"

"At the intersection with . . . South Spencer Field and Carlyn Lane."

"Then where did you and your brother go?"

"We ran down Carlyn Lane and then we went to a subdivision called Brentwood . . . Went to the very back of that subdivision in the woods and we just stayed there. Hid."

"And how long were you there?"

"Two days. Well, two nights, actually."

"And today's Tuesday the twenty-seventh. How did you get back to Pensacola today?"

"One of Rick's friends called him on his cell phone at the, at the convenience store that we just walked . . . that we walked up to."

"And did Rick come over and get ya?"

"Mm-hm." [Affirmative response]

"Where were you at when Rick came and got you?"

"In front of the convenience store on Ninety and East Spencer Field."

"So Rick . . . Y'all get in Rick's car. What's the conversation in Rick's car? What are y'all talking about?"

"He said he knew that something like this was gonna happen and he was gonna call Reggie so we could, so he could take us over here." Derek was referring to Deputy Reggie Jernigan.

"Over here. You're talking about over here at the sheriff's office?"

"Yes."

"Is there anything else that you'd like to add or take away from this statement?"

"What statement?" Derek asked.

"The statement you just gave."

"He just, he told us that he called some friends and tell them to be on the lookout."

"You talking about Rick?"

"Rick's, Rick's friends."

". . . Is there anything you'd like to say? . . . You can say anything else you want to say. Is there anything we forgot to ask you that you think is important?"

"I don't think so."

"Is there anything, any questions you'd like to ask us? Anything . . . You can ask anything you want to ask, we're gonna keep the tape on until you're ready for the tape to be turned off."

"I ain't for nothing else to say."

"John, do you have anything?" Kilgore asked his partner.

"Yeah," Sanderson responded. "As far as this interview today, when we've spoken to you, have we been fair to you?"

"Yes, sir."

"Have we threatened you in any way?" Sanderson asked.

"Hm-mm," Derek responded in the negative, indicating that he had not been threatened.

"Have you felt threatened?" Sanderson asked. The line of questioning, the detectives felt, was important in solidly establishing the facts of the case, in part to ascertain whether anything Derek told them had been fabricated and to show to others who would read the report that the statement had not been coerced. It was also important in the event that Derek's statement differed from his brother's, or if he changed his account later on.

"No."

"Okay, but did I ask you when you first came in if you were comfortable?" Sanderson asked.

"Mm-hm," Derek responded affirmatively.

"I'm not trying to put any words in your mouth," Sanderson added. "You tell me like it is, okay?"

"If you're not comfortable, say you're not comfortable," Kilgore said.

"I'm comfortable," Derek reiterated.

"Okay. Everything's fine?" Kilgore asked again.

"Yes, sir."

"Is there anything you'd like to ask us? Anything you want to know before the tape gets turned off?" Kilgore asked.

"No, sir."

"Is everything you told us the truth?"

"Yes, sir."

"You had talked when you got to Rick's house . . . Let me bring this up. You talked about when you got to Rick's house today that you changed clothes. Is that correct? Do you remember what you were wearing Sunday night, early Monday morning?" Kilgore asked.

"Mm-hm," Derek responded, indicating that he did remember.

"What was that?"

"Light blue shirt, black pants."

"Are those the same shoes that you were wearing?"

"Yes, sir."

"You wore those that night?"

"Yes, sir."

"Do you remember what your dad had on?"

"Uh, faded blue jeans. That's, that's all I can remember. . . . Maybe his jacket."

"What kind of jacket would that have been?"

"Black. It was a black jacket and I forgot what it had on it. . . . It had some, some kind of writing on the back of it."

"What about your little brother?"

"White shirt . . . that's about it. . . . All I can remember."

"Is there anything else you'd like to add or take away?"

"No, sir."

"Okay. John?"

"That's it," Sanderson replied.

"This concludes the recorded statement being taken at the Escambia County Sheriff's Department," Kilgore stated. "The time is seventeen-thirty hours. Thank you."

CHAPTER 6

Immediately following Derek's taped statement, Detectives Sanderson and Kilgore brought Alex into the interrogation room and questioned him at length about the events surrounding his father's death. It was about 6:20 P.M. when the questioning began.

"Pull your chair up a little closer to the desk so we get your voice, okay?" Kilgore asked. "Present also is investigator John Sanderson, ID number 154, assigned to the major crimes unit at the Escambia County Sheriff's Office, Homicide Unit. I'm Investigator Terry Lee Kilgore, ID number 146, assigned to the Major Crimes Unit with the Escambia County Sheriff's Department, Homicide Unit. All right, Alex, what we want to do is advise you of your Miranda rights again. Okay?"

"Okay," Alex responded. Like his brother, Alex seemed comfortable with the detectives, having developed a positive rapport with them prior to the taping of their official statements. Detective Kilgore read Alex his rights as he had with Derek, and confirmed that Alex had signed the same waiver.

"Alex, how old are you?" Kilgore began.

"Twelve."

"What grade are you in in school?"

"Sixth."

"You know how to read and write. Is that correct?"

"Yes, sir."

"And that you're a pretty smart guy," Kilgore stated matter-of-factly.

"Yeah."

"You know what's going on, right?"

"Yes, sir."

"You know the difference between right and wrong?"

"Yes, sir."

"What we want to do is talk about what happened at your house. And the address is 1104 Muscogee Road. And today's date's the twenty-seventh, and that's Tuesday . . . and what we want to talk about is Sunday night, which is the twenty-fifth, into the early morning hours of the twenty-sixth, which would be Monday. Okay?"

"Yes."

"What I want you to do is kind of start about what happened," Kilgore said. "I understand that you had been, that you had run away from home."

"Yes, sir."

"We had looked at a calendar earlier and I told you, because you weren't sure what the date was, but I told you that you ran away on a Friday and that would be November sixteenth, is that correct?"

"Yes, sir."

"Why don't you tell me about what happened Sunday right before you got uh, picked up? You turned yourself in from running away. . . . Tell us what happened. And I need you to speak up so we get everything on tape, okay? 'Cause you talk kind of soft."

"Yeah. All right. . . . What happened Sunday."

"Now this is when Rick came and picked you up."

". . . Sunday. . . . That was the first time we ran away?" Alex asked.

"Yeah, the first time," Kilgore responded.

"Derek . . . I went to explore the woods while Derek, um, he wanted to go to a friend's house to make a phone call, so I went to explore the woods to wait for him to come back and, uh, so whenever I came out of the woods, I looked . . . He hadn't shown up yet, and I looked for him, and I couldn't find him. So I figured that he had got caught and so, but I didn't want to turn myself in without that being the reason he didn't come back. And so I just, I spent the night in the woods waiting for him and he didn't show up. And so, I went to the Tom Thumb and I called Rick 'cause I didn't know any other number I could call, really. And so I decided I would just call Rick and he came and picked me up and, uh, while we were waiting, I was talking to my grandmother, Joyce Tracy, um, so we went, went across the street, McDonald's, to get something to eat 'cause I was hungry. And after a while, went back across the street, after a while, Terry and Derek showed up. I was talking to Derek about what happened. He told me, he filled me in on, uh, uh, what had happened whenever he got caught. He had called someone and, uh, the ladies had picked him up. Then they had called the police and come pick him up and, um, then he was taken to Terry."

"Now when you talk about Terry, Terry's your dad. Is that correct?" Kilgore asked.

"Yes, sir."

"Okay, go ahead."

"But biologically he is not my dad," Alex clarified. "He's not my father. Biologically."

Kilgore and Sanderson raised their eyebrows. There was nothing from official records or from the police interviews that had so far been conducted to substantiate any truth to this claim. However, Alex would later state that Chavis had told him that he was not Terry's biological son. If true, it was not known whether Chavis's purported statement had been made to poison Alex's mind against his father, or whether he was just telling him for the sake of telling him, or had let it slip. On the other hand, if the statement were later determined to be untrue, it may have been made up by Alex for reasons that might not ever become clear. Kilgore and Sanderson decided just to leave it alone for now.

"Okay," was all Kilgore said, and urged the boy to continue.

"So, after that, we, we went to the flea market to take the flyers down. . . . Of the missing persons. . . . Me and Derek."

"You and Derek had run away?" Kilgore reiterated.

"Yeah. . . . And, uh, so we took the flyers down, then we went to visit a friend of his, Mike from the flea market. And so while we were there, I was, we were talking about what would happen when we got home. And uh, we were talking . . . we were sort of talking about him dying a little bit."

"Wait a minute now. 'Dying a little bit'?" Kilgore interrupted.

"Well, him dying. We was talking about it a little bit, but it was about him dying."

"What was the conversation about?" Sanderson asked.

"Pretty much it was like I was saying, I was scared about what would happen whenever we got home and I couldn't really handle it that much longer. So, so we brought up the subject about his death, about, well about us killing him. So, but we went home and . . ."

"Did you talk about how you were gonna do it?" Sanderson asked, point-blank.

"No. Not then."

"Not then? Okay. Go ahead," Kilgore said. "So how long did y'all talk about that?"

"Not too long. . . . We just went back to talking about Corvettes, because that's my favorite car, so . . . We started on that," Alex continued. "And so we went, while we were there we horseplayed for a while. It was pretty late whenever we went home. It was in the night. And whenever we got home, he took a picture of Derek and of me and, uh, before we went inside [the green room] I went to use the restroom and Derek went in the, in his room to play. He played. That was, um, that was before we took our . . . It was after we took our shoes off. . . . I think we took our shoes off. . . . So, then I, I noticed that Terry was in the green room. I went in there and then, well, he called me in there and then he asked, he started asking why I ran away and I was saying, 'Because of what happened.' "

"And what happened?" Kilgore asked.

"Well, the day that we ran away, before we went to the, to the school, he, he threw us around, and before we went to school that day, we couldn't take it anymore because we had, um, we had, well, we had, he had done that before and, uh, he had done that before to us, um, so . . ."

"Now you talk about 'He's done it before,' " Kilgore said. "I mean, what do you talk about him doing?"

"Abuse," Alex answered, straight and to the point.

"Well, what type?"

"Mental and physical. . . . Mental, he was staring us down every time we got in trouble. He was using, um, extreme eye contact."

"Extreme eye contact? Staring you down. Okay."

"And, um, I had grown to where I could easily defend myself against that, which was rather simple because it's something dealing with the mind," the 12-year-old said. "Pretty strong in that aspect."

"Here you're pretty strong with that aspect of the mind, aren't you?" Kilgore asked.

"Yeah."

"So you could, you didn't have any problems with . . . the mental [aspect of the alleged abuse]?"

"No. . . . But Derek did. . . ."

"What about the physical abuse? You talked about that. What was he doing to ya?"

"Well, he threw us around, and whenever we were in the car, he, um, we said something that we weren't supposed to or something like that, when sometimes he'd hit us and he'd tell us to shut up."

"When he hit you, how would he hit you? I mean, how did he hit you?"

"Well, he hit me a couple of times. It wasn't very often that he did, but he hit me a couple of times with the back of his hand, well, basically slapped me across the face."

"The times that he'd slap you across the face, and you say that he didn't do it much, was it because you were in trouble, or something had happened, or what? Were you being disciplined?"

"No. He was, um, he must have had a bad day and I just, was talking and he hit me and told me to shut up [Inaudible] a couple of the times. I think that was all the times he hit me. Wasn't very often."

" 'Wasn't very often'?"

"Not at all."

"Let me ask you this. We were talking . . . earlier about being spanked for being disciplined. . . . Did the times that you were spanked, was it because you got in trouble for something you weren't supposed to do?"

"Yes, sir."

"All right. Tell me about that one time."

"The one time that he did use a stick, it was a long time ago, I got in trouble and he used the stick."

"How big was the stick?"

"I can't recollect that. It was too long ago. I was pretty young back then."

"You don't know if it was a little switch or if it was a big stick?" Sanderson asked.

"It wasn't, wasn't a little switch. I know that."

"That time, and then the other times you talk about, it's because you had done something wrong. Is that correct?" Kilgore asked.

"Yeah. It was. He used his hand a few times, most of the time he just used the belt."

"How many times did he whip you with the belt?"

"Well, I don't remember. I got in trouble so many times. I don't really remember."

"Was it because you were doing something wrong . . . is why you got in trouble?"

"Yeah. That's why. Mm-hm. He'd spank me with the belt, but that's a long time ago . . ."

"Do you remember how many times you been whipped with a belt?"

"No. It was quite a few times."

"How many's 'quite a few'?"

"I don't know. Well, more than just like, I think it was like ten or twenty times."

"Ten or twenty times, and that's just been recently?"

"No. Well, once recent, pretty recently. It wasn't till, well, it was a couple months ago that he hit, that he spanked me with a belt last time he did it."

"So that's the last time he spanked you?"

"Yeah."

"So you're over at Mike's house and you're talking about . . ."

"Talking about, well, I was saying that I was afraid of what would happen when we got home and, um, it came up that we, we, um, that about killing him came up next."

"How did it come up?"

"Well, I was, we was talking about what might happen when we got home and . . ."

"What did you think was gonna happen?"

"Well, we thought that he was gonna spank us then . . . and use the mental abuse and physical."

"Now you weren't too worried about the mental abuse, were you?"

"I wasn't worried at all about the mental abuse."

"Because . . . ?"

"It got to where it had no effect on me. . . . So

when we got home, um, took our shoes off, he [Derek] went in our room to play, played around for a while. I went into the bathroom and when I came out, Terry called me into the green room. He was talking about it and then, um, we were talking about it, and he grabbed me by the wrist and he threw me onto the ground, but my arm hit something. I can't recollect what it was 'cause I was, you know, in motion. I was looking at the ground. . . . But, uh, I hit something with this arm."

"And you're pointing to your left arm."

"Yes."

"Okay. You have to describe everything because the tape can't see."

"All right. Yeah. I'm pointing to my left arm and on my left wrist. . . . And near my elbow I have a mark from the impact."

"We'll take a digital picture of that with our camera, okay? Go ahead. What happens, what happens after that?"

"After that I run from the room, you know, I go in our room, there . . . and then we went back in our room and I told him what happened, and me and Derek, we share a room, and we had the front of the house. . . . We talked about what had happened and, um, told him what happened and so . . . Said that we wished that he was dead."

"Who said that?"

"I said that," Alex responded. "I said I wished he was dead and, um, I don't know who said it, but said that, one of us said, made a comment that we, why don't we kill him? It's like, we said that we have us, I said, you know, we need something to stun him, use the knife 'cause the, the knife might not penetrate the first time and, uh, and I said we could use a hammer and, uh, that is, if we use a knife. We went back to the worktable which was at the back of the house."

"Your bedroom's in the front of the house?" Kilgore asked.

"Yes."

"So you already talked about killing Terry," Kilgore said. It was more of a statement than a question.

"Yeah."

"And you walked back to the back, to the worktable?"

"Yeah."

"Why did you go back there?"

"To look for a hammer."

"To kill Terry?"

"Yeah. To kill Terry. So we looked for a hammer. We couldn't find one and, uh, he pulled the bat out. I think he used that, you know. I thought about it and I figured out that it would be a better choice, so we took the bat into the green room. By that time he was, uh, I believe he was only pretending to sleep 'cause it had been a long time since he had done that. So I think he was only pretending to sleep, which would be real likely because it does take him a minute to go to sleep, if— We weren't talking that long, not that long."

"Okay."

"So he, he hits him with a bat the first time. Sounds about like wood cracking or . . . hitting concrete or something. Then he misses the second time and he hits the lamp, takes, turns it off. I was standing, well, there's a couch, um, in the back of the green room, not the back of it, but there's a couch to the left of the green room. Well, as soon as you walk into the green room, to the left is a chair and um, that's all that's on that wall. Then . . . a little bit in front of the chair is a table. I was standing at the far end of the table from Terry. And so he hits him and the third time the bat makes contact with his head. Blood comes from [his head] and he keeps hitting with it. Then, um, we run, we run from the room."

"What are you doing when Derek's hitting him with the bat?"

"I was just standing there watching him."

"Now, how far are you from Terry when he's getting hit with the bat?"

"Maybe ten meters, possibly."

"Do you know how far a meter is as versus a foot?"

"Three feet."

"Okay."

"Twelve times three is thirty-six."

"Thirty-six."

"Thirty-six inches."

"Well, a meter is a little further than thirty-six inches," Kilgore corrected.

"Yeah, a little bit further because it's metric," agreed Alex. "There's a little difference between them. And, um, so it's like about a couple meters."

"A couple of meters from him. Okay." Terry Kilgore nodded his head in understanding.

"And then, uh, he hits him with the bat a bunch of times, I think it's about ten or fifteen times, and then [we] run from the room and, um . . ."

"Hold on," Sanderson interjected. "And describe the injuries. Earlier, you described the injuries."

"All right. The third time it made contact, blood come from his head. . . . Then he smashed, he smashed his face in. His skull, well, normally his skull, it, uh, his forehead is in line, was, well, his nose comes out further than his forehead normally, of course, his normal size head, but whenever he smashes his face in is smashed in further than his head, and he knocks a hole in his head. It's smashed to the right, Terry, 'cause the left is, um, he hits him and the bat makes contact with the left side and, uh, makes contact with the forehead, knocks a hole in the forehead, you could see his brains. . . . Then we run from the room, run to the, by the worktable, at the beginning of the worktable into the left is his room. We throw the bat onto the bed, then we run back to the other end of the house and we throw our shoes on real quick. Then, um, by that time we were getting kind of panicky because of the fact of what we did. It just hit us, and so we ran back into the bedroom and, uh, we lit the bed using [Inaudible] and lighter for the fire because it was an old house and it burns easily. We knew this."

"Whose idea was it to set the fire?" Sanderson asked.

"Derek's."

"How did y'all get that idea, and why did y'all do that?" Sanderson asked.

"We got the idea because it, the house itself is very flammable, and we got, and we decided to do that because of the evidence, it would destroy the evidence and we were real, real worried about getting caught and everything," Alex replied.

"Who'd y'all learn that from?" Sanderson probed.

"Blue lights."

"Blue lights" was an apparent reference to police-related television shows, and was how they referred to them in general.

"Is that where you learned that from?" Sanderson asked.

"Yeah. We thought that wouldn't be too good of an idea to get caught, well, to have it all just right there, obvious what we did, so we just lit the house on fire. . . . And besides, he was in there. The noise he made the first, the noise he made, the first impact was a groan and, um, he squeezed his eyes shut. You could tell that he was in pain, and he missed the second time. The third when he, the second time he made contact, which was the third time he swung, uh, I think it knocked him out, but the fourth time he swung, the third time he made contact, the blood came from his forehead, so I knew he was out. By the time he got done, he was still trying to breathe and, uh, made sort of like a sound like the person has a slightly stopped-up nose, made that sort of a sound and every time he breathed out, well, the times I saw this, um, his face, the skin on his face sort of puffed out from the air. [Inaudible]"

"Now why do you think that?" Sanderson asked.

"Um, I was scared and, uh, I was feeling . . . I don't know."

"Is there anything to do with the fire as far as worrying that he may be still be alive?" Sanderson asked.

"No . . . but it was obvious that he was dead. . . . Well, not dead, but 'cause of the way he was breathing we didn't know if he was dead or not, but I knew he was already there, he had to be there, 'cause a little bit of his brains was on the wall, I believe."

"How did you feel about that?" Sanderson asked.

". . . very disturbed and very scared, and so we set the house on fire."

"Did, did you ever think about calling 911? Calling help for Terry?" Kilgore asked.

"No."

"Why not?" Kilgore asked.

"Well, we thought he was already dead or . . . on his way, and so we didn't really think about calling for help, and, well, the situation, um, we were so scared and everything like that, so . . . We decided that, we just ran from that. We lit the bed on fire— it was a small fire from what I saw—we went in the house and wait, and waited a little while longer, but whenever we ran past the bedroom for the second time, well, we went past the bedroom the first time after we put the bat in there and lit the fire, I didn't look in because I was just wanting to get to the back door, because that was the easiest to open, so we turn, we twisted . . . there was a little piece of board on the bottom that has a nail on it to where you could twist it to stop the door from opening and above, near the window, which, it has four square window, which is divided into four even squares . . . there's a little lock, I don't know what you call it. I think it's a latch of some sort. . . . But, um, you know, it's, it's a long line, it's a little metal cylinder and it has a little handle and you push it up and push it over and push it down again."

"I know what you're talking about," Sanderson stated.

"Some sort of a latch," Alex continued. "And when you twisted the handle, after we undid the latch, we twisted the handle and pulled it, and noticed the board was there and I twisted it and opened it up and we, there's another little latch thing for the screen where it has a hook that slides into an eye. We popped that latch open, we opened the door and ran from the house. We ran right and then took a right as soon as we exited the yard and then there's . . . past the neighbors' house, right beside the neighbors' house, there's a street and we took that right, it was also to the right. We ran down that way. And then we ran and walked, we did a mixture of both. Ran, running, walking and jogging. We got to the Three Mile Bridge and we hitchhiked across it."

"Now is that the Three Mile Bridge you're talking about or is that the bridge on Nine Mile Road going into Pace?" Kilgore tried to clarify. "Or Highway Ninety? Now, see, Three Mile Bridge, when you say that, that's the one going from Pensacola to Gulf Breeze."

"The beach area," interjected Sanderson.

"Yeah, that is Gulf Breeze, but I don't think it was the Three Mile Bridge. I think it was a different bridge," Alex said.

"Was it the interstate bridge or were you on the interstate or were you just on the four-lane highway going toward Milton and Pace?" Kilgore asked.

"I don't really know. . . . I wasn't really seeing what we did," Alex replied. "We did catch a ride across the bridge, whatever bridge it was."

"Okay."

"And then there was . . . in the woods there's a trail that led to a little canopy-type thing. I think it's a canopy or a tent, a tent-type thing that we spent the night in before . . . the first time we ran away. And so we . . . stayed there for a couple nights."

"Let's go back real quick to the workbench," Kilgore said. "What you had talked about earlier . . . There was some lighter fluids and stuff. Tell us about that."

"All right. There's uh, two cans of charcoal lighter, some, there's this off-brand type in a metal container, and there wasn't much in it, and there was, uh, there was another type, a better type that was in a plastic container. We didn't use any of it. [Inaudible] We just lit the bed 'cause we knew the house was very vulnerable because it was so old, didn't know exactly how it was burnable, but we just knew that it was and so we just lit the bed. The bed had several blankets, different blankets on it, so we knew that it would be a good igniter itself."

"There were other fluids in the room right next to this room," Sanderson interjected. "Is that right?"

"Yes."

"You mentioned something earlier about y'all leaving and y'all had a conversation about the car," Sanderson said. "Tell me about that."

"About the car? Uh, his [Terry's] car?"

"Uh-huh," Sanderson said. "Terry's car."

"We had a conversation about it," Alex replied. "I'm trying to remember what it was . . ."

"Do we need to kind of refresh your memory?" Kilgore asked. "We don't want to put words in your mouth."

"Yeah, you can."

"You talked about maybe taking Terry's car," Kilgore reminded him.

"Oh yeah."

"Do you remember now?" Kilgore asked.

"That was just so minor," Alex said. "We thought about it, but it's like, 'No, that would be too obvious, two teenagers, two, a teenager and a pre-teen driving a car.' "

"Y'all talked about that?" Kilgore asked.

"Well, not really talked about it, we just mentioned that, and it's like, 'No, that'd be too obvious.' "

"Okay. Is, is there anything else?" Kilgore asked.

"Well, after, we spent a couple of nights and then we couldn't handle it being [Inaudible-noise] couldn't handle knowing about it anymore, so we just called. Derek got one of his lady friends to call Rick, Rick Chavis, on the cell phone and so he picked us up by the Tom Thumb, around the Tom Thumb, but he picked us, picked me up before, so . . . Then we went to his house. We got cleaned up. We took a shower and then, um, we, we, uh, waited for Reggie to come pick us up and take us here."

"And 'here' is the sheriff's office, right?" Kilgore asked.

"Yeah, the sheriff's office."

At that point Kilgore advised Alex that the tape had turned off and had been off for approximately fifteen seconds. The detective asked him to repeat what he had just told them during that time frame, which Alex did.

". . . and so on the way to Rick's house, we, um, talked about, me and Derek . . . both took turns telling Rick what happened . . . so far as Terry's death and . . . what led up to it and whenever we got to Rick's house we each took a shower and, um, we cleaned off our clothes," Alex added.

"Why'd you do that?" Kilgore asked.

" 'Cause of, uh, it was a mess. We didn't really want to look so ragged, you know. . . . Look a little bit more presentable. So we cleaned off our clothes a little bit and so, waited for Reggie [Deputy Jernigan] to pick us up, take us to the sheriff's office."

"And that's how you ended up here," Kilgore stated.

"Yes, sir."

"Are these clothes that you've got on now—it's a white tee shirt and blue jeans and a pair of white tennis shoes—are those the same clothes you wore when . . . over at Terry's house that night?" Kilgore asked.

"Yes, sir."

"These are clothes that you wore when Terry died?" Kilgore clarified.

"Yes."

"Do you have the same socks on?" Sanderson asked.

"I don't have any socks on. I didn't wear them."

"Were you barefooted that night before you put your shoes on, or did you have socks on?" Sanderson asked.

"Before I put my shoes on I was," Alex responded. "Well . . . I didn't put socks on . . . I took my socks off at Terry's house and then I put my shoes back on because . . . I wanted to spend as little time as possible in that house, so . . ."

"You know Rick for a long time?" Sanderson asked.

"Uh, yeah."

"If anybody was to say Rick was involved in this in any way, did Rick know . . . until you told him, did Rick know anything about what happened that night?" Sanderson asked. "Did he know beforehand it was gonna happen? Did he know right after?"

"He knew," Alex responded. "I don't think he

knew anything beforehand, uh, he said that he felt that it might come down to this, but we didn't tell him about it beforehand. After what's happened, a couple of days, then he knew about it, because we didn't contact him. After we ran away the first time and I don't, I don't believe we made any contact. The reason I say that is because of Derek. Don't really know what happened, that is, a few times we did get separated or we were separated . . . and so Rick, we didn't contact Rick except to come pick us up. He picked me up the first time in the same . . . [Inaudible] . . . both of us up."

"As far as the death of your father, did Rick know before it was gonna happen that it was gonna happen?" Sanderson asked.

"He didn't know for a fact, but he had a feeling that it would," Alex replied.

"How do you know that?" Kilgore asked.

" 'Cause he told me about it. Out there they were talking about it."

"Out where?" Kilgore asked.

"Right out there in the waiting area."

"You talking about today?" Kilgore asked.

"Yeah. Today he said that."

"What was he saying?" Kilgore asked.

". . . I was just talking stuff and, uh, he said that I, we weren't really talking about that, just talking about odd stuff, like a conversation instead of being bored. . . . We were just making conversation, so I told Reggie that I had a feeling it might come down to this. And so he, um, he said, it was like Reggie said that he'd have to be listening to him more often."

". . . Did Rick come over there the other night?" Sanderson asked.

"No."

"Did he give y'all a ride anywhere?"

"No. He had no involvement in it as far as anything . . ."

"If anybody was to ever say Rick was involved, that Rick helped y'all, or Rick was there, or Rick gave y'all a ride from there, if anybody was ever to say that, would that be true?"

"No. That would be false information."

"As far as this interview that we just had . . . okay . . . we were fair toward you?" Sanderson asked.

"Yes," Alex replied.

"Did we threaten you in any way?"

"No."

"Did you feel comfortable with us or did we make you feel uncomfortable or . . ." Sanderson trailed off.

"I was comfortable."

"As far as this rights form, did we explain it to you in a way where you understood everything on it?" Sanderson asked.

"Yes."

"Let me ask you this," Kilgore cut in. "How do you feel about Terry's death now?"

"I have a mixture of feelings, really. The same, uh, as I had. Well, after I calmed down, it was just, I developed a mixture of feelings which I still have."

"Can you describe those for me?" Kilgore asked.

"Yes. Um, I feel a little sad about it, a little sad, a little bit, um, a little relieved that we don't have to go through it, go through what he put us through again, the abuse and, uh, a little bit, mainly, uh, mainly I feel kind of down about it. Because of the fact that, you know, it was a death and I saw it and it's just kind of real disturbing."

"Okay, well, do you feel responsible?" Kilgore asked.

"Yeah."

"For his death?"

"Yes I do. I feel mainly responsible. Derek, Derek took the hits and, but I was the one that gave him the idea."

"You're the one that gave Derek the idea?" Kilgore asked.

"Yeah. I feel I'm more responsible than Derek, really. I mean, 'cause the fact that I gave him the idea and all."

"Let me ask you one other thing," Sanderson said. "As far as Terry, I know you were talking about the mental- and the physical-type abuse and all, and it was sparse . . . I mean, it was here-and-there, it sounds like it. Was it or not?"

"The mental abuse . . . It started a long time ago and had been going on for a real long time . . . I got informed by someone that he was doing this and so . . ." Alex said.

"Who informed you of that?" Kilgore asked.

"Um, I don't really want to say."

"Well, no, you need to tell us who informed you of it. It was Rick, wasn't it?" Kilgore asked.

"Mm, yeah."

"Rick said that he was mentally abusing you?" Kilgore asked.

"Yeah, he told me that, um, that, well, we had talked a lot and we were good friends and, uh, he said that he'd done mental abuse and he told me about it and then I started getting stronger towards him 'cause, uh, I knew what it was, and I found a way to just sort of deflect . . ."

"Before Rick told you that, did it . . ." Sanderson trailed off, waiting for an answer.

"It affected me big-time."

"It did before that?" Sanderson asked.

"Mm-hm." [Positive response]

"But now, it didn't bother you now?" Kilgore asked.

"No. . . . It has no effect."

"Because you're mentally stronger," Kilgore suggested.

"Yes. Towards what he's doing."

"As far as clothing you and feeding you and everything, how was, how was Terry as far as that?" Sanderson asked.

"Well, he was, um, very good. He did a lot for me. He was, uh, he kept me well fed and, um, clothes, we always had good clothes on and so, but, uh, sometimes when he got bad, it was hard to get the food, but we went through those times."

"Did he try the best he could, do you think?" Sanderson asked.

"Yes. We had snack cakes that we had gotten, we had gotten some snack cakes from places. He bought snacks, so . . . We lived off those for a couple of times."

"Did he buy you toys?" Sanderson asked.

"Yeah. We had a lot of toys."

"Buy you a lot of gifts? Things like that?" Sanderson asked.

"Yeah. . . . He was good at that."

"Did he take you out to do entertaining-type things?" Sanderson asked.

"Not much at all. One time . . ."

"Did you go out to eat a lot?" Sanderson cut in.

"We went out to eat. That was basically our thing, 'cause we didn't stay at home, you know. We went out to Chuck E. Cheese's once. . . . We did have a TV for a while but . . ." Alex trailed off.

"Did it break . . . ?"

"No. He got rid of it, but it's been a while now since I've seen TV, except for at Rick's house. He, he's been very reclusive. . . . Very, very reclusive. . . ." [Alex apparently referred to his father being reclusive.]

"You haven't been enjoying it," Kilgore stated.

"Yeah. . . . We didn't have much entertainment at the house. Just some books that I read about a thousand times and, uh, he had that and a couple of board games, but as far as the entertainment there, we didn't have much at all."

"You talk about Rick being a good friend," Kilgore said. "Did you used to write a lot in your diary? Do you have a diary?"

Kilgore was fishing. He recalled Sanderson's interview with Lewis Michael Tyson regarding diaries that Terry King said he'd read, and wondered aloud if any such diary had been written by Alex.

"I don't have one," Alex replied. "I did have one for a while but I really was never good at writing down my thoughts and my feelings. I can say them a lot better than writing them. I couldn't write them down. . . . I never could figure out what to write, so . . ."

"Has Rick been a good friend to you?" Kilgore asked.

Again, Kilgore was speculating. Recalling the digital camera and photos that Terry had spoken to Tyson about, as well as Chavis's intense interest in the boys and the case, Kilgore could not help but focus on Chavis.

"Yeah. He's a good friend. He's been good for me. He helped me out some on, so far as Terry, you know, and he's . . ."

"Has he helped you out on some other things?" Kilgore probed.

"Well, learning. He's helped, I watched him do a lot of these, a lot of his stuff and his work and he's explained it to me, so he's helped me out on that and, uh, and, uh, as far as Terry, what Terry was doing, so . . ."

"All right, John, do you have anything else?" Kilgore asked.

"No. I don't think so," Sanderson replied.

"Is there anything you'd like to add or take away from this statement?" Kilgore asked Alex. "Anything else you'd like to say?"

"Uh . . . no. I don't believe so."

"Okay. This concludes the recorded statement being taken at the Escambia County Sheriff's Department," Kilgore concluded. "The time is nineteen–twenty-three hours. Thank you."

CHAPTER 7

Following the interviews with Detectives Sanderson and Kilgore, Alex and Derek King were placed under arrest and each was charged with an open count of murder in connection with the death of their father. Being charged with open counts of murder meant that it would be left up to the prosecutor or a grand jury to determine whether the charge would be first-degree murder, second-degree murder, and so forth. A conviction of first-degree murder carried a possible life sentence in Florida, even for juveniles. Florida, for reasons that aren't quite understood by much of the rest of the country, often treats juveniles as adults, sending them away for life and leaving little hope for rehabilitation.

For example, in July 2001, Nathaniel Brazill, 14 years old when he shot and killed his teacher in Lake Worth, Florida, was convicted of second-degree murder and sentenced to 28 years in prison. Six months earlier, in January 2001, Lionel Tate was convicted of first-degree murder and sentenced to life in prison for the slaying of a 6-year-old girl in Pembroke, Florida. Tate was only 12 years old when he killed the girl.

Following their interviews, both Alex and Derek were taken to the Escambia County Jail where they were fingerprinted and photographed. Afterward they were taken to the Department of Youth Services, across the street from the sheriff's office, where they were incarcerated and held without bond. Only a few months behind Tate in age, Alex and Derek King became the youngest murder suspects in Florida history.

Under Florida law, according to Assistant State Attorney Dick Schoditsch, murder cases must be brought before a grand jury before they can go to trial. If the grand jury hands down an indictment, the age of the accused becomes inconsequential. Children would be charged as adults and, if convicted, sentenced as though they were adults.

"In other cases," Schoditsch said, "such as lesser felonies, depending on the age and prior record, there is much more latitude whether or not to file as an adult or as a youth. But any time they go to a grand jury, then they are forever treated as adults."

Earlier, when the boys mentioned that their clothes had been washed, Deputy Reggie Jernigan briefly left the sheriff's office and went to Rick Chavis's residence. He recovered and bagged as potential evidence the clothes that the boys said had been washed there. Also, the clothing the boys were wearing at the time of the interviews was confiscated at their bookings, to be examined for potential evidence.

According to what few details were initially released to the news media following Alex's and Derek's arrests, one major avenue of the homicide investigation concentrated on where the two brothers had gone after their father was killed, and how they managed to get to their destinations.

"How did these kids travel at one A.M.?" Escambia County Chief Deputy Larry Smith asked reporters as he publicly pondered the situation. "How'd they get from here to there? How did they stay out of sight for this extended period of time?" Smith, with twenty-five years of law enforcement experience in Florida, told reporters that Alex and Derek were the youngest suspects charged with murder that he had ever encountered. "We just need to make sure that, in the course of our investigative activities, that when we're dealing with someone this young, we pursue it in a very cautious, but very direct manner, to be able to accomplish the task."

As details of Terry King's murder began making headlines and charges were filed against his boys, more and more people across Florida and the southeastern U.S. expressed shock over the case. Chief Circuit Court Judge John Kuder, who told reporters that he had been following the case closely, echoed Chief Deputy Smith's statements about Alex and Derek being the youngest people charged with murder in Florida. "It's something that rarely, rarely happens," Judge Kuder stated. "This is very unusual."

Officials at Ransom Middle School chimed in and said that they had never had any problems with Alex and Derek.

"They were withdrawn and kept to themselves," Principal Richard Harper said. "But they just seemed to be normal middle school kids. I'm in a state of shock."

"He was just a nice kid," said Joe Murphy, a physical education teacher at Ransom who knew Derek. Murphy described Derek as a pleasant and seemingly happy boy. "Nothing out of the ordinary about him. Nobody could have ever suspected something like this would happen."

At 11:15 A.M. on Wednesday, November 28, Detective John Sanderson contacted a Santa Rosa County deputy who had picked up Derek on November 24 on Highway 90. While in the car, Derek apparently told the deputy that his dad would not allow him or Alex to watch television or to have friends over, and that was one of the primary reasons that he and his brother would run away from home. Derek, who told the deputy that he wanted to be an engineer when he grew up, stated that his father was mentally abusive to both him and his brother, the Santa Rosa County deputy told Sanderson. The deputy stated that Derek said Alex was at one of his dad's friend's homes, and that Derek had described the friend's home as having a security system. He also said that Derek had told him that his dad's friend was a convicted felon.

At the time the Santa Rosa County deputy took custody of Derek, the boy was found to have cigarette lighters in his possession. Derek also stated that his father used to smoke marijuana. When the deputy arrived at King's home, he told King much of what Derek had told him, prompting King to defend himself.

After finishing with the deputy at 12:45 P.M., Sanderson received a telephone call from Kelly Marino, formerly Janet French, Alex and Derek's mother. After displaying shock and disbelief about everything that had occurred up to that time, Marino explained how she had been with Terry King for eight years. She described him as being of good character and said that Terry was not mentally abusive toward the boys and would not have hurt them physically, either. She claimed that he adored both of them and "spoiled them rotten." She said that when punishment was needed, Terry was consistent. She did not provide details of the type of punishment that was used when warranted. Marino told the detective that she would be traveling to Florida soon and promised that she would contact him again when she arrived.

Later that afternoon Sanderson and Kilgore went to the Brentwood subdivision located near East Spencer Field Road, where Alex and Derek claimed that they had gone into hiding. They found the lake area that the boys had described in the rear of the neighborhood where a covered hut of sorts was situated. They carefully photographed the area, then proceeded to canvass the neighborhood. As they went from house to house, some of the neighbors reported seeing Terry King the day before his death, searching for his sons. However, the detectives could not find any kids in the neighborhood who had seen either of the boys, and none of the kids the detectives spoke with knew anything about Alex and Derek.

Shortly after 5 P.M. that same day, Sanderson drove to Lewis Michael Tyson's home, simply to check the mileage from Tyson's residence to the King residence on Muscogee Road. Upon leaving Tyson's home, Sanderson went to Fairfield Drive, then east on Fairfield N to W Street. He then traversed north on N W Street to Highway 29, then north to Muscogee Road. Upon reaching Muscogee Road he drove west until he reached the King residence. Having observed the speed limit during the drive, and taking note that the traffic was relatively light and that he was stopped at very few traffic signals, Sanderson noted that it had taken him twenty-nine minutes to make the 17.2-mile journey. He further noted that in all likelihood, traffic would have been lighter late in the evening that Terry King and his boys had visited him. Given the time frame that Tyson and others had related to him, in which King and his boys had left his house at 12:15 A.M., there would have been ample time for King and the boys to arrive home, and for the tragic turn of events to have occurred within the time frames that had been established by the investigating officers and fire department personnel.

CHAPTER 8

When John Sanderson arrived at work early the next morning, he learned that the official autopsy report surrounding Terry King's death had been issued. The autopsy had been conducted on Monday afternoon, November 26, by Gary D. Cumberland, M.D., a forensic pathologist and the chief medical examiner for Florida's District I, and John Holland, also of the medical examiner's office. Although the official autopsy had been conducted on Monday, and seemed to confirm investigators' initial suspicions, the official report was not presented until after all the tests had been conducted on King's organs and fluids and the results of those tests were known.

The report indicated that Terry King was a normally developed 40-year-old who appeared his age. He measured 5 feet, 4 inches tall and weighed 123 pounds. There was obvious trauma to the body, particularly the head and face. King's hair was about two and one half inches in length, black with gray, and he wore a mustache. It was obvious that he had not shaved for several days because of the beard stubble that was present on his face and chin. When brought to the morgue, King's body was clothed in a long-sleeved green camouflage jacket, a white tee shirt bearing a horse emblem, and white Jockey undershorts.

The victim had clearly suffered major trauma to the head. In addition to abrasions on the scalp, there were the more serious injuries comprised of fractures to the skull, as well as marked hemorrhages in the soft tissues of the scalp. Injuries to the area of the front of the head, more to the left side than the right, and to the nose could also be observed. After the pathologist removed King's brain, he could easily distinguish marked contusions and hemorrhage present in a number of areas or regions.

At the conclusion of the definitive autopsy, Dr. Cumberland's pathologic diagnoses were that King had died of blunt force injuries to the head. He labeled King's death a homicide, and the cops called it murder.

After reading the report that morning, Sanderson interviewed Kevin Bailey, the legal owner of the house at 1104 Muscogee Road where King had lived with his sons. Bailey told the detective that he had known Terry King for about five years. He said that he had purchased the house in January 2001 and that King had moved into it on February 1, not during the summer months as some of the neighbors had initially told investigators.

"I really bought the house for Terry," Bailey stated. He said that King did a great job of keeping the house up, and that Alex seemed to be very proud of it.

According to Bailey's statement, he had last spoken to Terry King on Wednesday, November 21. Terry told him that he had begun experiencing disciplinary problems with Derek right after the boy moved in with him and Alex. Bailey stated that Alex became less cheerful after Derek moved into the house. He said that Alex resented the fact that Derek could smoke cigarettes but that he could not. Terry told Bailey how he had been in touch with the sheriff's office after the boys ran away, but was not getting any help. Terry also told Bailey that someone had given the boys a ride to the Pace area, where they claimed to have been hiding out.

Though the boys were known to go to Sunday school and both looked like choirboys, Bailey told the detective that he suspected that Derek might have been involved with a gang. Perhaps because of a detective's intuition, Sanderson wanted to know if Bailey knew anything about Chavis's relationship with the boys or their father.

The boys never talked about their friend Rick, and Bailey was unable to offer any useful information about their connection to him. He said that he had never known Terry to have had a girlfriend in the time that he had known him, nor had he ever seen him in the presence of a woman. He said that Terry never spoke of any problems at home until Derek came to live with them. Bailey said he knew that Terry had spent a great deal of time with Alex, and felt that he was a good father. He had never known Terry to hit or strike either of the boys, but Terry had told him that he had to occasionally raise his voice to them after Derek moved in.

Bailey said that Alex had always called Terry "Dad," but recently had begun calling him by his first name. Terry apparently told Bailey of a message that had been left by Alex on Rick Chavis's answering machine after the boys had run away from home in which Alex had stated: "Terry, I'm not coming back." According to Bailey, Terry was intimidated by Derek.

At approximately 11:50 A.M., after the interview wrapped up, Sanderson and Kilgore went to the evidence garage where they examined items inside Terry King's car, including various papers. Identification Officer Jan Johnson, who had collected evidence at the King residence in the hours after the slaying, met the two detectives at the garage and turned over some items that she had collected, among which were notes that had been compiled in a spiral notebook that she had found in the house's attic. The book could have been construed as a diary of sorts written by Alex. As they read the handwritten passages which began, "Biography—Do not read!," the detectives raised their eyebrows as they realized that the case was suddenly becoming more complex.

"My life used to be cloudy before I made friends with Rick," read the journal. "Rick let me see what I didn't understand. Life isn't about having a job. Life isn't about importance. Fame. My ultimate goal in life now is what his is. It is about sharing your life with someone else. Before I met Rick I was strate [sic] but now I am gay."

Other notes read: "Alex David King loves Ricky Marvin Chavis so-so much always and forever," and "I love you so so much and I will always love you." Yet another note read, "I love you Rick." Alex King had signed the documents.

Sanderson and Kilgore looked at each other and

each could almost tell what the other was thinking: What was the depth of Chavis's role in this case? Had their intuition about Chavis been on target? They each decided that a thorough search of Chavis's home was in order, as was a thorough background check. If that document had been the one that Terry King had talked about with Lewis Tyson, it was no wonder that King had harbored feelings of fear toward Derek. Reading those kinds of words from one's own son were enough to make a parent fear that his boys were plotting against him, perhaps aided by a pervert bent on preying upon children, a man he had once considered a good friend.

When they returned to the sheriff's office, the detectives entered Ricky Marvin Chavis's name into their computer system, along with his date of birth, October 7, 1961. In a matter of moments complaint number 930545 popped up, detailing a charge against the 6-foot, 3-inch 175-pound man with green eyes and brown hair. He had been 23 years old at the time he was charged with "lewd, lascivious or indecent assault or act upon a child," and a second charge of "procuring minors for prostitution." He had been employed as a security guard at a motel at the time. The alleged offense involved Chavis and two juveniles.

The complaint alleged that "on January 13, 1984, in the late night hours . . . one Ricky M. Chavis did suck the penis of [juvenile witness's name deleted] without his expressed or implied consent. This act was witnessed by [juvenile witness's name deleted]. The . . . [victimized] juveniles [were] on a runaway status at that time. While at the Chavis residence the juveniles were given shelter, food, pot, beer in exchange for sex. All three (3) persons were using the same bed to sleep on." Chavis had pleaded no contest in 1984 and had been sentenced to six months in jail for the molestations. The crimes that he had committed, as well as the sentencing that he had received, had all occurred at a time when sex crimes were treated less seriously than they are today. In today's courtrooms, Chavis would be looking at years, not mere months, for similar crimes against children.

The detectives suddenly realized that Chavis's prior acts gave his relationship with the boys a particularly creepy sheen. How far had he gone with Alex and Derek? Because of his prior conviction, the detectives, who are accustomed to predicting present and future behavior based on one's past behavior, feared the worst.

As they prepared their affidavit for a warrant to search Chavis's residence, they recalled how Chavis had first told them that an unknown female had called him on November 27 to tell him where he could pick up the boys, after which he claimed that he had taken them home with him and called the police. A short time later, they recalled, he told them that he had met the boys at a convenience store at approximately 1:40 A.M. on November 26, which would have been immediately after the discovery of King's death. And on yet another occasion Chavis had told the investigators that he had had Alex and Derek with him on November 16, after they had run away from home. He also said that he had taken Derek to see a girl in nearby Santa Rosa County on November 24, near the location where deputies eventually found the boy and took him home to his father. The following day,

Chavis had returned Alex to his dad, only hours before Terry King was killed.

So why had he made the conflicting statements? the detectives wondered.

A short time later Sanderson and Kilgore obtained their warrant and searched Chavis's home in a thorough and methodical manner. The weapon used to kill King had not been found at the scene of the crime, but it was believed to have been a baseball bat because of the severity of King's injuries, as well as because of Alex's and Derek's statements. At one point the detectives found a broken aluminum baseball bat, red in color, but they could not immediately determine whether it was the murder weapon. They also seized computer hardware and software, as well as drug paraphernalia. The computerware would be carefully analyzed for evidence that might shed light on King's death, and for child pornography. Anything found would likely not be revealed until the case went to court.

They also found a photograph of Alex that had been hanging over Chavis's bed, as well as a letter that Alex had written to Chavis.

CHAPTER 9

Chavis's potential role in the case was becoming more and more obvious, particularly after the police found Alex's notebook in which he had written that the convicted child molester had encouraged him to become a homosexual. Sanderson and Kilgore now decided that it would be prudent to look more into Chavis's life and mode of living. When questioned again about his lifestyle, Chavis confirmed that he was a homosexual, but claimed that he had not been involved in a physical relationship with anyone for several years. However, the detectives soon learned that his home, located in a Pensacola trailer park, was purportedly known as a hangout of sorts among the neighborhood kids. The detectives learned that many of the local children often watched television and played video games there.

Throughout the preliminary stages of the investigation, Sanderson and Kilgore contacted Dennis Shuman, an attorney who had been assigned to represent Alex King shortly after Alex's arrest. Shuman met the detectives at the Juvenile Justice Center where photographs were obtained of injuries to Alex's wrist. Sanderson had written in his notes that on the evening that he and Kilgore interviewed the boys, the only injury they had observed was to Alex's left wrist, which was pointed out during the interview. It had purportedly been incurred when Terry King threw the boy to the floor, causing Alex to strike his wrist against an object—he couldn't recall what—on the way down.

At another point early in the investigation, the boys' mother, Kelly Michelle Marino, came into the sheriff's office just as she had promised that she would. She again repeated how she and Terry King had never married, and that after their breakup several years earlier, she had married a man and moved to Kentucky where she went by the name of Janet French.

French told Sanderson that she had met Terry King in 1985 and they remained together for approximately eight years. She related how she had remained with Derek until he was five years old, at which time he went to live with the Lays. She stated that she had two other children, twins, with another man, but that Terry treated them like they were his own. She said that she left because of financial problems, that it was very tough getting by with six people in the family. Even though she claimed to love her children dearly, she said the stress of their situation at the time caused her to "freak out," meet someone else and leave in 1994. She said that Terry had kept all of the children, and the financial difficulties continued for him. At one point he had heard about the Heritage House, also known as the Heritage Christian Academy, for children, and decided to place the children there. The crisis home no longer exists.

The academy's director, Reverend Steve Zepp, kept all four boys at the home for approximately eight months and eventually suggested that they be adopted out or placed in foster homes.

"He explained to us that sometimes the best thing to do for your children is to give them up," French said. "I know a lot of people are saying stuff, but it hurt me, and we had to do what was best for our children. Those people [who are saying things] aren't in my shoes. They don't understand how hard it is to care for four boys under those conditions."

When Derek moved in with the Lays in 1995, Alex was sent to live with another family at about the same time. However, Alex did not adjust to his new home and began "pitching fits," crying all the time and demanding to stay with his father. The new family felt that things would just not work out with Alex, and the boy was returned to his father about a month later. The Lays wanted to keep Derek, and it was agreed that they would. French said that although she left Terry in 1994, she had remained in Pensacola until 1998 and often visited Alex, as well as the twins. However, after visiting Derek at the Lays' on and off for about a month, she did not see him again until he was incarcerated in the Escambia County juvenile facility.

Derek's relationship with the Lays lasted until September 25, 2001, when they contacted Terry and said that they could no longer keep the boy. They said that he was out of control, that he was sniffing lighter fluid, that he had a fascination with razor blades, and purportedly used them to cut up his mattress. According to French's statement, the Lays said that they were afraid Derek might harm one of their grandchildren if he remained with the family.

"Nancy [Lay] told me that Derek had been disrupting their lives so much," French said. "Apparently it had become awful. She told me they'd tried everything in the world to help him, but it just wasn't working out."

French said that moving to the rural area of Cantonment had been hard on Derek. He'd had a lot of friends while living at the Lays', and had been actively involved in church. The move had been more difficult for him than anyone had thought it would be.

"I talked to Terry at work and he said that it wasn't going too well," French said. "Derek missed his friends, and it was just hard adjusting to a new place with someone who was pretty much a stranger."

French told Sanderson that Derek had ADHD, attention deficit hyperactivity disorder, and was on the medication Ritalin for a time. At one point, while still with the Lays, he had begun taking a new medication for the condition. She stated that after the boy moved back home with his father and brother, Terry had problems with him at first because Derek apparently missed the Lays. Shortly after Derek moved back home, Terry took him off his medication and he seemed to be doing better because of that, according to conversations that French said she'd had with Terry. Derek and Alex were playing well together and their grades at school had improved. Terry told French that he felt that Derek hadn't needed the medication after all.

She said that, judging from conversations she'd

had with Terry, things had seemed to improve during the last few weeks prior to Terry's death, until the boys ran away from home. She said that Terry hadn't celebrated Thanksgiving because he had spent the day searching for the boys. He even took time off from his job so that he could look for them, to no avail.

At one point, she said, Terry had told her that Derek and Alex were grown-ups in children's bodies. She wasn't quite sure what he meant, but on other occasions he told her that Derek had a fascination about drugs, mushrooms, how to make bombs, snorting Ritalin, and making bongs, skills he had apparently learned from some of his older friends who were in high school. Reportedly, when Derek would listen to music on his stereo, his personality would change for the worse and he would begin acting differently than normal such as becoming more disrespectful to his father and others. At some point Terry apparently made the decision to take the stereo away from him, and made the boys stop watching television. Terry told French that there was something, she didn't know what, that the boys had been picking up from television police shows that apparently had caused Terry some concern—he was afraid that they might apply whatever it was to their actions.

Was Terry just being paranoid? the cops wondered. Or was there something more sinister that he had learned about that caused him to distrust his sons?

French said that Terry was strict with the boys, but was never abusive and rarely ever raised his voice to them. She described how Terry would make Derek breakfast every morning at Derek's request. She said

that Terry was quiet, was of good character and
stayed to himself most of the time.

"Not one part of that man was controlling," French
said. "He was quiet, passive, not loud. He didn't have
a mean bone in his body. He adored his boys. He
loved them so much." She said that Terry and the
boys had been putting up Christmas decorations prior
to King's death.

On the various occasions when she had spoken
with Terry, he would talk about his friend Rick. On
one of those occasions she said that he and Rick had
been teaching Alex and Derek tae kwon do because
the boys had been getting picked on at school. On
another occasion Terry apparently told French that he
did not like it when Alex had once said that he
wanted to live with Rick when he grew up.

French also told Sanderson that her mother and
stepfather, the Walkers, would "butt into" her and
Terry's business and had called the authorities on
them once because they were trying to gain custody
of their grandson Derek. French stated that Rick
Chavis had told the Walkers that he wanted to adopt
Alex, but this was before anyone knew that their supposed friend had a record for crimes against children.
She said that Terry and Rick would communicate to
each other using a walkie-talkie because Terry didn't
have telephone service.

French told Sanderson that when she had met with
Alex and Derek at the juvenile detention center she
had asked Derek, "Why did you do what you did?"
She said that Derek merely shrugged his shoulders.
The boys told her that Rick Chavis was a good friend.
When she asked Alex about the mental abuse he had
claimed to have received from Terry, the 12-year-old

said that he hadn't known it was mental abuse until Rick had told him that it was. Alex had been referring to the so-called mind control, the staring that they claimed had been going on.

When she asked the boys what they had done for Thanksgiving, they told her that they had stayed in the woods in Pace. Derek also told her that he had felt bad about what they did to their father, and that was why they had turned themselves in, or had arranged to do so through Rick Chavis.

Alex told his mother that Derek cried a lot. "I'm worried about Derek," French quoted Alex as saying to her, "because he doesn't know how to phase out the pain . . . I've already cried. Now I just phase out the pain."

Later, French spoke with local reporters about her initial visit with Alex and Derek at the juvenile detention facility.

"They had their backs turned to me when I walked in," French told a reporter, "and I just thought, 'Those are my children?' It felt like I was in some dream. It was unreal."

Although she had not seen either of the boys for at least three years, she visited with them for about thirty minutes shortly after arriving in Pensacola from Kentucky. She sat across a table from them in a visiting room.

"Whatever happens now, their lives are ruined," she said. "I was sitting there talking to them, and they were still the sweet, loving boys I always remember. Just looking at them, remembering the little boys we played with and raised . . . I told them that I loved them, that I always have, and I always will. I told them how much it hurt me to be away from them, but I explained to them that we thought we were doing the best thing for them . . . I just can't picture my little boys committing that horrible crime . . . I'm not sure what I'm going to do now. Part of me wants to stay here and do whatever I can, but the other part of me tells me to just stay away. But I realize that this isn't something that you can just put behind you. This is going to take a long time, and I just don't know what to do."

CHAPTER 10

As John Sanderson and Terry Kilgore continued their investigation into the violent death of Terry King, they spoke with people who'd known him, those who had worked with him, those who had gone to Derek's church, and so forth. By Friday, November 30, they had logged nearly 120 hours on the investigation, and it was not anywhere near the point where it would begin winding down.

Those who knew King told the detectives that they considered him strict, a man who carefully guarded his family's privacy, but none of the people the detectives spoke to had foreseen any indication of the violence that was committed.

"We knew Derek was a troubled child," said Reverend Ted Traylor, pastor of Olive Baptist Church in Pensacola where Frank Lay is a deacon. "But my goodness, never in my wildest imagination would I have thought that it would come to a charge of murder to two young boys. It just blew us all away. We just weren't looking for it . . . Derek was a rambunctious young man like others. He could be rebellious, but no more than other children."

Reverend Traylor did not know Terry King, or Alex, and had little to say about Derek leaving the Lays' to return to his father's home. He stated that Derek never indicated to him that he did not want to go. He said he had held personal sessions with Derek and the Lays prior to the boy's departure that indicated the depth of some of the problems that they were having.

"I have just known some of the agony with Frank and Nancy," Traylor said. "I have a pastoral confidence with some things there, having prayed with them and encouraged them. It was tough."

At one point Sanderson went to Pace Printing, Terry King's last place of employment, where he spoke with co-workers. Jim Collie, 47, a pressman like Terry, told the detective that he had known Terry for nearly ten years. He said that he had observed that King was strict with the boys.

"I don't know if you'd call it discipline or punishment," Collie said. "I would say it was more of a punishment nature. I never seen him strike them or anything, but he definitely made them walk the line."

Collie recalled an occasion in which King had come to visit him at his home and had brought along both boys with him. Later, on another occasion, King had come to visit and had only brought Alex with him. When Collie inquired about Derek, King only told him that Derek had gone to live with his mother.

"I said, 'Well, he's [Alex's] not living with his mother?' He [Terry] just very sternly said, 'Hell, no.' That was the end of it. I knew then not to push the issue."

Even while socializing Terry never had much to say about his private life, according to Collie. "If you asked him [something about his private life]," Collie said, "sometimes he would just give you a blank look, and that was just letting you know that it wasn't any of your business." Collie said that he never saw anything, and King had not told him anything, that would have caused him to believe that there was any discord between King and his boys. He said that he'd seen nothing to lead him to think that a homicide might occur.

Pace Printing's owner and Terry's boss, Skip Sisley, described Terry as a quiet man, but diligent in his work. "He was steady," Sisley said. "I could always count on him." He recalled that Terry often brought Alex to work with him. "The boy would sit in the break room and either color, do homework or read a book."

When police interviewed another friend, Joseph Tibbles, who said that Terry and Alex lived in his home for a year in 1997 when they were having a particularly difficult time getting by, he had observed a very well-mannered boy in Alex and a loving father in Terry. He said that he had never heard Terry raise his voice to the child.

Asked whether King was a control freak, Tibbles replied, "He was always very protective of his boy, but never controlling. I've seen him give anything just for his son to have something." Tibbles said that his 13-year-old daughter often played games with Alex, but neither she nor Tibbles ever heard Alex say anything bad or inappropriate about his father. Tibbles said that Terry was a diligent man who'd had a string of bad luck in his life, but that he never gave up in the face of adversity.

"He always worked so hard," Tibbles said. "He was always trying to get that one foot forward."

When Sanderson checked King's background, he found that he did have a criminal record. But though they could not say for certain whether there was psychological abuse, as the boys had claimed, King's criminal record was totally unrelated. He had a history of passing worthless checks, driving under the influence and driving with a suspended license.

As for Alex and Derek, Sanderson confirmed that both boys went to Sunday school, and that Alex was doing reasonably well in his classes. Alex's sixth grade math teacher, Marilyn Bridges, said that Alex was such a bright student that she decided to move him into a more advanced math class. She said, however, that after she moved him, she noticed a change in him. "He was doing much better at the beginning," Bridges said. "Then he slacked off. Alex was very quiet and didn't raise his hand too much. He was well behaved."

Another teacher, Herman White, who was Derek's physical education teacher, described Derek as "smallish" and characterized him as a good runner. White said that Derek finished the mile run in less than seven minutes. White said that he was surprised that the boy had been accused of murdering his father. In his twenty-seven years of teaching, White said that he would never have considered Derek as the type who would commit such a crime.

At Terry's wake, the victim's father, Wilbur King, continued to try to make some sense out of what had happened.

"We don't understand," King said. "Derek and Alex are just like any other boys. They like fishing, playing video games, TV and stuff like that."

"I don't have a clue why this happened," echoed the Reverend Paul Welch, pastor of the First Pentecostal Church in Pensacola. "I don't think anyone can explain why."

Terry King was buried on Friday, November 30, following services at Faith Chapel Funeral Home.

In the meantime, Terry King's former friend Rick Chavis came forward in an interview with the local newspaper, the *Pensacola News Journal*, in which he described King as a "control freak or a power freak." Chavis had asked the newspaper not to reveal his name, but as the case moved forward, it became obvious that he was the person who'd provided the interview. He said that King did not allow Alex and Derek to have much outside contact with others. He claimed that the boys had told him that they felt psychologically abused, and that Alex had told him that he wished that his father was dead.

"I said, 'You don't wish death on anybody,' " Chavis told the *News Journal*. "He said, 'I'm so tired of being abused.' "

"They're basically good boys," Chavis said. "It just got to a point where they couldn't handle it. They just simply got fed up and couldn't handle it." Chavis said that he believed that the boys' complaints about their father were legitimate ones.

Chavis attempted to characterize King as a strict and controlling man. After Derek moved back home, Chavis said, King had nailed the windows shut and had installed locks on the doors that required keys to operate them.

"I told Terry that he didn't need to nail everything shut, for fire reasons," Chavis said.

According to Chavis, Terry King allowed Alex and Derek very little interaction with other people. While he worked swing shift at Pace Printing, 2 P.M. to 10 P.M., he insisted that the boys remain inside the house after arriving home from school until he could pick them up at approximately 5 P.M. and take them back to the printing plant. Derek had been accustomed to being active in school, church and sports leagues, and the new rules of inactivity were difficult for him to deal with emotionally.

"Derek said that he couldn't handle it," Chavis said. "He was used to having an outgoing life, being with kids his own age. Terry wouldn't let him. The sudden shock of being cooped up in the house every day was too much for him."

Alex, Chavis said, was used to that lifestyle. However, Alex eventually became resentful after Derek moved back home and took away some of the attention that Alex was accustomed to receiving from his dad. He said that when Terry gave Alex attention, it was negative attention.

"Terry used to stare down Alex real bad," Chavis said. "One time in my living room, I didn't notice Alex doing anything bad, but Terry yelled at him so loud that I even jumped . . . I tried to pick up the slack with Alex. I told Terry, 'You need to pay equal attention to the boys and treat them the same.' He said, 'No one is going to tell me how to raise my boys.' "

Chavis told the newspaper that approximately two

days after King's slaying, he'd received a telephone call from an unknown woman. He said she instructed him to drive north along East Spencer Field Road in nearby Pace. "The boys saw my car and came out of the woods," Chavis said. "I stopped, and they jumped right in. They didn't say nothing at first. Then they said, 'We're so glad to see you.'"

Chavis said that he took Alex and Derek to his home, and then called a deputy with the Escambia County Sheriff's Department, whom he characterized as a friend, and turned the boys over to him for transport to the sheriff's office.

Chavis said that he never suspected for even a moment that the problems the boys claimed they were having with their father would end in a slaying.

"It was bad enough that I knew why they ran away," Chavis said. "But I never figured that they were even capable of murder."

Chavis recounted some of the difficulties Terry had endured after Alex and Derek's mother left them, including how Derek had gone to live with Frank and Nancy Lay.

"Terry couldn't take care of both boys," Chavis clarified.

Chavis said that neither Alex nor Derek provided many details of the killing to him. He told the paper that he did not know where the boys had been hiding from the time that Terry King had been killed until the time he had received the mysterious telephone call from the unknown woman. He said that he assumed that they had been hiding in the woods. He stated that the boys seemed to be frightened when he picked them up, and they cried occasionally, but neither of them seemed to understand the legal consequences of what they had done. He said that he told them he would do whatever he could to help them and that he hoped he would be able to testify on their behalf when the case made it to court.

"I told them, 'Y'all are about to be in for some serious tough times,' " Chavis said. " 'All I can do is be there for y'all.' "

CHAPTER 11

"Just about as normal a kid as you could get," said Mike Bradford, a building contractor in Pace, Florida, characterizing Derek King. Bradford had been Derek's coach in a basketball league for young people. Bradford said that he never saw any red flags at all, and that Derek was a kid who nearly always went out of his way to be amiable.

"Derek seemed to pop up everywhere," Bradford continued. "For all the years after I coached him, he'd run up and say, 'Hey, Coach Mike, how's it going?' I would characterize him as a sweet kid."

Although Bradford did not know Terry King or anything about him, he held the Lays in high regard and said he felt that Derek was lucky to have been able to live with them.

"Frank would bring Derek to practice," Bradford said. "Sometimes he would stay for practice, but he would always pick Derek up afterward. I think a lot of Frank Lay from what I've seen and how he handles situations, and all I thought was, Derek was with Frank Lay, therefore Derek was in good hands."

As additional background on Alex and Derek and their home life began to emerge, it was nearly always the same: shock and disbelief that these cherub-faced boys could have actually perpetrated the type of crime for which they'd been charged.

"I've watched Derek grow up these last few years," said Reverend Ted Traylor to reporters for the *Pensacola News Journal.* "He's just full of life and vinegar, with those eyes just flashing. He's energy to the tenth power . . . it's tragic. It's unthinkable . . . It's just numbing to us. This child carried more baggage than any of us deserve, but there had to be some extraordinary circumstances for this to happen."

Many of the 8,000 members of Olive Baptist Church were adversely affected by the murder charges. A lot of those who spoke about the boys were moved to tears. Reverend Traylor said that Derek was well-liked by the adults and the kids, but he and Associate Pastor Stan Lewis both admitted that Derek had problems that stemmed from his family background. He could sometimes be unruly, they said, just like other boys his age. They felt that he was similar in many ways to any number of children who had similar family problems in their backgrounds.

"Derek has a scarred heart," Traylor said. "So he might be a little more rebellious than other kids." Traylor said that it was his perception that Derek was always looking for affection. "He was reaching out for what he didn't have. He longed for . . . relationships. You could sense that in him."

"He's a little boy with a tough package of emotions who has gone through some things that no little boy should have to go through," said Dave Paxton, one of Olive Baptist Church's youth ministers.

"Derek is just fun and energy personified," said Stan Lewis. "He's never-met-a-stranger personified . . . he's all about people."

Nearly all of those at Derek's former church agreed that he was a good-natured kid who was popular with other children his age.

One 12-year-old girl who attended Olive Baptist Church and went to school with Derek at Sims Middle School characterized him as a Bible scholar. She said that he always seemed to be trying to comfort other kids who had problems. The girl said that Derek loved his father and, although he regretted having to leave his school and church friends behind, had seemed genuinely happy when he learned that he was going to move back home to live with his father and brother. She said that she had only seen him become angry when someone said anything bad about him or his family. The girl said that she was stunned when she heard about Terry King's slaying and the fact that Derek and Alex had been arrested for it.

"That's not the Derek I knew," she said.

Another former classmate of Derek's, a 13-year-old girl, characterized him as someone who was fun-loving and liked to go to school. He particularly liked to go to the Heartbeat Café, a hangout at Sims Middle School where the kids could buy Cokes and candy and sit around and talk to each other.

"If the doors were open, he would be there," said the girl. "He was fun to be around. He made lots of jokes. He was a good kid."

The principal at Sims Middle School, Wanda Knowles, was acquainted with Derek during the two years that he attended classes there. She said that his disciplinary problems were not too serious, mostly little things that would result in a trip to the office.

"I know he was a pretty sharp kid," Knowles said. "He was very capable and bright. I would classify him as average to above average in class . . . I know it sounds cliché, but he was just your average middle-school student . . . he never did anything you would call major or out of the ordinary. At least nothing to give anything like this away."

Reverend Steve Zepp, formerly director of the Heritage Christian Academy, held similar feelings about the boys.

"When they were with us," Zepp said, "they were typical boys being separated from their parents. They were just average little boys. We were just there to give them unconditional love and structure in their lives . . . they were hurting little boys . . . [who] needed more than he [Terry] could give them."

Zepp thought very highly of the Lays, and stated that he had been happy about their decision to take in Derek. "Those are the finest people you will ever meet," Zepp said. "I know they're torn up about all of this."

King, while trying to work and make a living for his boys, had been attempting to home-school Alex prior to enrolling him in Ransom Middle School. The decision to enroll him came about after Derek returned to live with Terry.

"It about breaks your heart," said Kathryn Bryan, 66, a neighbor. She said that she had made attempts to get acquainted with King shortly after he moved into the house on Muscogee Road, but he resisted. She offered Alex a ride to her church, but King declined it. "My son said to me, 'Mom, I wish you

could have said more and maybe the boys would
have come to you. Maybe the boys would have told
you what was going on.'

"We never did see him playing and having fun like
a child would," Bryan continued. She said that King
"worked like a dog" in the yard trying to make his
home look nice, and Alex was always right there beside him, helping him. "But we thought, Well, he's
dad's bud, he's dad's clone."

John Carroll, who worked at Pace Printing with
Terry King, told reporters what others had said,
namely that Alex regularly went to work with his
father and stayed in the lunch room. He said that
Alex mostly read Harry Potter books, colored, or
played games on his Game Boy. Sometimes he would
just sleep, creating a makeshift bed by sliding the
chairs together.

"The reason that a situation like that worked out
in a place of business," Carroll said, "was because
Alex was such a well-behaved kid."

"The situation was never a problem," agreed Skip
Sisley, the shop's owner and King's boss. "I just assumed it was kind of hard being a single dad to find
a day-care center that was open at night. So I let it
slide . . . He [Alex] was here more than he wasn't.
Some nights he'd sleep in a sleeping bag . . . The boy
never caused a problem and there was no mess in the
morning."

Sisley told reporters, along with Sanderson, that
he never had a clue that there was a problem at home
or that one was brewing. He said that the first time
he knew of anything wrong was when King came to
work on Friday, November 23, and told him that
Alex and Derek were missing. He asked to take the

day off so that he could search for them.

"I didn't question him any further after he told me that," Sisley said. "He said he knew of a couple of places to look for them, but I didn't pry into it."

"I knew about the boys missing, too," Carroll chimed in, "but I reacted like everybody else did. Shock . . . He [King] seemed worried the last couple of weeks, but we're kind of upset that he didn't talk more than he did. We wish we could've done more to help out."

Wilbur King, Terry's father, indicated that he would make an independent effort to find his son's killer, because neither he nor any member of his family believed that Alex and Derek had done what they were accused of doing.

"We don't believe the boys did it," King said. "No one can understand any how, or why, about any of this. They were a close family, and he loved those boys." King, who said that he sent his oldest son, Greg, to visit the boys in jail, said that he and his family were having a very difficult time with what had happened, and that their faith in God was the only thing that was helping them through the ordeal. "At night it weighs heavy. We are a drained and distraught family. We suffered grief this week and we just don't know why."

Meanwhile, as Assistant State Attorney David Rimmer began putting the case together for presentation to a grand jury, Reverend Steve Zepp began making plans to visit Alex and Derek at the juvenile detention facility where they were jailed.

"Maybe, when the investigation gets through," Zepp said, "we can make some better sense of this tragedy. But if they did what they're accused of, there's just got to be some kind of explanation. Knowing the kids the way I did, I can't fathom them doing this. There's got to be something more . . . there's got to be something more."

If the grand jury returned indictments for first-degree murder, second-degree murder, or manslaughter, the two children would be automatically tried in adult court according to Florida statutes rather than juvenile court. An indictment would also cause the boys to be moved from the juvenile detention center to the Escambia County Jail to await trial. And if convicted of first-degree murder, they would be sentenced to a mandatory life term in prison.

CHAPTER 12

The police now knew Derek King was the boy who eagerly went to Sunday school and Bible study, and was a member of the church choir and the church's youth fellowship program. Was he the person who had swung the baseball bat that killed his father? What would have been the motivating circumstances behind such actions? The detectives could only wonder. It must have been more than the mere suggestion of his brother, Alex, who had stated that he'd wished his father were dead. Or was it?

According to experts who study the cases of children who kill their parents, such slayings are often the result of a severe family breakdown or prolonged abuse by one or both of the parents. Paul Mones, Portland, Oregon, lawyer and the author of the book *When a Child Kills*, said there are approximately 200–300 incidents in which children kill a parent each year in the U.S. Approximately one-half of such killings are committed by those under the age of 18. But what are the motives for such killings?

"Maybe some killed for money, or because they

couldn't use the family car," Mones said. "But the overwhelming majority are responding to abuse and extremely dysfunctional families"—roughly seventy percent, according to Mones. "Most of these kids don't have the same profile as kids who kill strangers. They tend to have average to above-average intelligence. They're polite. They obey adults. They generally don't have a history of acting violently at all."

In many cases juveniles are convicted on lesser charges than first-degree murder. For instance, Conan Pope, a Nevada 15-year-old who killed his father in a disagreement about dirty dishes, was allowed to plead guilty to voluntary manslaughter and could be released from prison after four years or less. Pope, who had received extensive counseling prior to his sentencing, told the judge, sobbing, that he wished that his father were still alive. "But my family was not healthy," Pope had said. "It was filled with violence, fear, guns, drugs and abuse."

"The trend is to treat these kids as juveniles," Mones said. Except in Florida, of course. "And to give them some sort of treatment even if they are transferred to adult court. The research literature shows these kids are extremely well-suited to rehabilitation."

"It's easy to look at the parents and say it's all their fault," said Adam Weisman, a psychology instructor at Pepperdine University. "But you have to look at the dynamics. Is there prior juvenile delinquent experience? Has there been some knocking around of the parents, and the parents taking it because the kids have gotten too big for their britches?" Weisman's opinion is that authorities should remain open-minded as they investigate and judge cases involving children who kill their parents.

Kathleen M. Heide, author of the book *Why Kids Kill Parents* and a criminology professor at the University of South Florida, believes that there are three basic categories of children who commit such crimes: 1) children acting out of desperation following experiences of abuse or witnessing other members of their family being abused, by far the greatest category; 2) anti-social children who have become dangerous, often after having already been in trouble with the law—members of this group sometimes view one or both parents as an obstacle to their objectives; and 3) those who kill a parent because of a mental illness that has not been recognized and/or treated.

Where did Alex and Derek King fit into all of this? No one knew at this point. And it wasn't likely anyone would know until the boys had been through extensive counseling. But Heide offered that their behavior could have involved their exposure to an anti-social role model, Ricky Chavis, at a significant time in their lives.

"In other words," Heide said, "what was this man communicating to these boys? What sort of influence did he have? That's the part we don't know."

Heide also suggested the mental health experts would need to look at possible emotional neglect, since there appeared to be little or no evidence of physical abuse.

"There's the absent mom," she said. "The fact that the boy was in foster care for so long tells you something. Did the father maintain a relationship? Or has the child been abandoned? Emotional neglect could very definitely affect the child's ability to bond and to have a sense of empathy and connection with the parent. It could also mean that the child has hatred and rage toward the parents who abandoned him . . . there are [also] a lot of children who are abused who do not kill their parents."

"You don't know what this man [Chavis] may have said to turn the boys against their father," offered Dr. Diane Schetky, whose practice in Rockport, Maine, involves forensic child and adolescent psychiatry. "Given that they didn't spend a lot of time with their dad, you have to wonder about the strength of that attachment. It didn't take much for him to turn the children against their father, apparently."

Schetky suggested that Chavis may have tainted Alex's and Derek's impressions of how their father was raising them, and may have led them to perceive their father's attempts at disciplining them as a form of abuse. This would have encouraged the boys to resent his actions.

"It sounds like this pedophile [Chavis] was approaching them as a friend, not as an adult authority," Schetky said.

According to Rick Spencer, a developmental and child psychologist in Pensacola, the physical abuse that Alex and Derek claimed had occurred did not appear particularly significant. However, the possible mental abuse might be.

"Abuse is in the eyes of the beholder," Spencer said. "If the child perceives it as abusive, he may experience it that way or at least lead others to believe he's being abused in that manner. From the sound of the confession, the older brother certainly felt protective of the younger brother. Whether the abuse was reality or conceptual, we'll just have to find out."

Although it is normal for children to harbor momentary feelings of wishing that their parents were dead, it is necessary for a child to dehumanize or objectify the parent in order to distance himself from that parent and make the wish a reality.

"Alex had a longer time to be attached to his father," Spencer said. "Derek, who spent six years out of the household, would be less so. Then it makes sense why Alex was not the person who did the damage. It might make sense why he is the one to show more remorse right now."

Spencer compared the alliance between Alex and Derek to that of the two teenage boys from Columbine High School in Colorado, who killed thirteen of their fellow students before committing suicide in 1999.

"In the Columbine incident," Spencer offered, "a child feels picked on and rejected, but then talks to other kids who feel the same way. They form a group, then they develop this Trenchcoat Mafia, and it becomes a bit of a normal thing. You begin to dehumanize these other people, and then it becomes more of a possibility of acting out the fantasies because they're more normal. . . . We've got Alex, a twelve-year-old who has this relationship with a child molester. Alex is the one who has lived with his father the longest and may feel the most restricted because of his desire to be with this man."

The issue of how to prosecute and punish juvenile killers instigated a legal debate in Florida that focused on Alex and Derek King, particularly since they were the youngest children ever to be accused of murder in the state. The case quickly caught the attention of the rest of the country and prompted Florida legislators on both sides of the issue to enter the legal dispute. Senator Skip Campbell, a Democrat from Fort Lauderdale, was among the first to come out and complain that the penalties under the current statutes are too severe.

"We have to have a fair system," Campbell said. "For those children that do things off the cuff, emotionally, that can be rehabilitated, I'm not too sure that society will be benefited by keeping them in jail for the rest of their lives."

Campbell's idea of fairness involved having those juveniles under the age of 16 who have been convicted of a crime punishable by death or life imprisonment committed to a juvenile facility until they turn 21. At that time a hearing would be held in which a judge would rule whether the person has been reformed or not. If the person were deemed rehabilitated, he or she would be conditionally released on a probationary period of sorts. Those deemed not rehabilitated would be sentenced to life in prison, but would eventually be eligible for parole. Senator Victor Crist, a Republican in Tampa and chairman of the Senate Criminal Justice Committee, was quick to disagree with Campbell's plan.

"I think that approach is far too liberal," Crist said. "Murder is murder, and dead is dead. If somebody has killed an individual, then they don't belong in society. . . . If the child demonstrates that they can commit cold-blooded, heinous murder, the chances are, they're going to do it again and again and again.

It's time to look at the victims and their rights."

Florida's strict laws entered the national spotlight in 2001, prior to the Alex and Derek King case. Lionel Tate was only 12 when he killed 6-year-old Tiffany Eunick in July 1999 in Pembroke. Tate had claimed that he accidentally killed the girl while imitating professional wrestling moves. He caused injuries so severe that the girl's liver became detached. He was sentenced to life in prison without parole in January 2001.

Another Florida case that received national attention involved John Silva. Silva was only 15 when he strangled 12-year-old Jerry Lee Alley, Jr., on May 26, 2000. The victim's body was found in an Interlachen, Florida, septic tank. Silva was also sentenced to life in prison without parole in February 2001.

Yet another much-publicized Florida case involved Nathaniel Brazill. Brazill was 13 when he shot and killed a teacher, 35-year-old Barry Grunow, at Lake Worth Middle School, also on May 26, 2000. Brazill's defense was that he never meant to shoot the teacher—he had only intended to frighten Grunow with the gun because he had refused to allow the boy to see two girls in a class he taught. The gun, Brazill said, went off accidentally. Brazill was convicted of second-degree murder and sentenced to 28 years in prison. Under Florida law, he will be required to serve a minimum of 85 percent of his sentence before becoming eligible for parole.

"There are bad kids that probably should stay in jail the rest of their lives," Campbell said. "But I think there also are some very ill-fated kids that prob-

Terry King, the victim. Derek and Alex King, his sons, his killers. Rick Chavis, his friend, his betrayer. *Associated Press*

Kelly Marino, Alex and Derek King's mother, left,
speaks with Joyce Tracy, her former mother-in-law.
Associated Press

Joyce Tracy, Terry's mother, Alex and Derek's grandmother. Waiting in lawyer's office shortly after Alex and Derek's arrest. *Associated Press*

Jimmie Walker, the boys' maternal step-grandfather. *Associated Press*

Rick Chavis, at his trial for the murder of Terry King.
Associated Press

Escambia County, Florida, Circuit Judge Frank Bell, at Rick Chavis's murder trial. *Associated Press*

Chavis receives a congratulatory pat on the back from his attorney, Michael Rollo, after being found not guilty in Terry King's murder. *Associated Press*

Outside the Escambia County Courthouse in Pensacola, Florida, where media outlets from around the country set up to cover the murder trials of Chavis and of Alex and Derek. *Associated Press*

Alex and Derek King entering the courtroom. *Associated Press*

Kelly Marino shields her
face after the jury
returns guilty verdicts
against her sons.
Associated Press

Alex King, seated next
to his attorney, James
Stokes. *Associated Press*

Escambia County Prosecutor David Rimmer listens as Judge Frank Bell overturns Alex and Derek's convictions. *Associated Press*

Derek King, center, all smiles, with his attorneys, Dennis Corder, left, and Sharon Potter, right. *Associated Press*

Alex King, right, sitting next to his attorney, James Stokes, upon hearing Judge Bell's decision. *Associated Press*

ably, if you ask them to do it again, they wouldn't do it if they knew the consequences."

Did Alex and Derek King fall into that scenario? Only time would tell.

CHAPTER 13

Additional insight into the lives of the King family began to emerge when portions of Terry King's diary were made public by the *Pensacola News Journal*. The handwritten diary, which had been obtained by the Escambia County Sheriff's Department investigators during a search of King's house, was produced approximately six years before his slaying. It contained Terry's thoughts about Alex and Derek's mother, Janet French, as well as references to the disordered and sometimes frenzied family life to which the boys had been subjected.

"A lot of times people mistake children for objects of personal property," Terry had written. "They are not objects. They are little people with feelings and emotions, and those feelings and emotions are very fragile and should be protected . . ."

King talked about being frustrated with the boys' mother, Janet, who, according to the diary, would disappear for hours or even days before returning home. He was also frustrated at not being able to adequately provide for his family, and was troubled by his legal problems from the bad checks and from driving with a suspended license. He wasn't sure whether he would end up going to jail or not at the time he wrote of his frustrations. He also wrote about how he and Janet had lived together from 1986 through 1995, and how she had given birth to two other children, twins, fathered by another man.

"Over the past five years Janet would go through long periods of time that no matter how many or how few hours I would work she would tell me how hard of a day she had at home with the children and that she needed a break," he had written in the diary. "She would stay gone anywhere from two or three to six or eight hours. And in the past three years her time away from home ranged from three or four hours to all night till the next day."

He described how he had lost his job in 1993 and how the family had been evicted from their house. When he finally found another job, he was only paid $5 per hour. The need for more money prompted Janet to go to work as a dancer. He wrote that her job paid better than his job, which caused him to agree to stay home and take care of the kids. Over time, Janet began spending more and more time away from home, days at a time, until she eventually moved in with another man.

"We had little or no food, no money," he wrote. "And all four children were there with me wondering when she was going to come home. She claimed that staying gone those periods of time was such a relief from being a 'mommy.' And she loves to see them but she wished that she wasn't a 'mommy' because she doesn't want the responsibility of a mommy because it's too much work being at home with them."

Another section of the diary read: "Ever since the oldest was a little baby up until she left the first days of June '94, I was the one to get up with them at night, not Janet . . . I have been able to locate a safe home with Christian leadership and a very secure, comfortable atmosphere and environment for the children to stay until I am able to clear myself of the courts and establish a home for all four of the children to live in so the children and I can be together and grow together as a family . . . [Janet] is comfortable and satisfied with the fact that they are not with her so she doesn't have to be responsible for them at all times and don't interfere with her free time that she could spend somewhere else."

Terry wrote how Alex and Derek had gone to live with separate grandparents in 1994 when their mother had moved out of the house with her twins from the other relationship. Terry's final entry read: "The point of everything I am doing right now is to bring the family together with the exception of the mother."

Alex and Derek's maternal grandmother, Linda Walker, 51, who works as a deli clerk and lives in Cottage Hill, Florida, revealed a starkly contrasting portrait of Terry King and his family. "The boys haven't had a normal life, you know," Walker stated without hesitation. "They've been thrown around since the day they were born. Rejected by their mother. Rejected by their daddy. They're so starved for love. They're troubled children." She quickly dismissed any notion that the boys could have killed their father, however. "There's no way they could be violent. They're just not that type of kids. What they need is to go back to juvenile court and get the psychological help they need."

Walker stated that she was embarrassed by her daughter, Janet, who, she said, has very little to do with any of her four children. Much of what Walker had to say confirmed the entries in Terry's diary about their lifestyle and the hardships that they had endured.

"Lord knows where I went wrong raising that young 'un," Walker said of French. "She's my daughter, and we've argued over the years because of the way these kids got treated." Walker recalled how Janet had given birth to Derek in 1988, to Alex in 1989, and to the twin boys in 1991. She said that in addition to Janet discovering how difficult it was to be a mother, some of their other problems stemmed from the money they wanted to spend on their social lives and on Terry's hobby of repairing cars with his friend, Rick Chavis.

Those issues, as well as others, resulted in their not having sufficient money to survive on. As a result Walker said that she and her husband often gave them money for groceries and utility bills, among other necessities. There were also times when Terry, Janet and the boys would move in with Walker and her husband, but they would only stay a few months.

Janet, according to her mother, liked to stay up all night long and sleep during the day, making it difficult to get the children to school. Her solution to that problem was to keep the kids up at night, too, so they would sleep during the day when she slept.

At one point, when Derek was about halfway through kindergarten, he was permitted to move in with Walker. Janet and Terry signed documents that had been notarized, agreeing to turn Derek over to Walker, but the actions were never confirmed through any court of law. A few months later, when Derek was about to begin first grade, his father picked him up for a visit and never returned him to his grandmother. A short time later, Derek and Alex were placed in the Heritage Christian Academy. Eight months later, Derek was living with Frank and Nancy Lay. Although Alex had also gone into a foster home, he was returned to his father for a time. But when King was unable to handle him, Alex moved in with Walker's ex-husband and lived there for approximately two years before going back to his father. As the boys were being moved around, Janet, according to her mother, went from one relationship to another until she married and moved to Kentucky. According to Walker, Janet has since divorced the man and has married again.

When Derek came to live with her, he was considerably behind a typical kindergartner's development, according to Walker.

"I felt so sorry for him," Walker related. "His mother and father wouldn't give him a bath, and he was unkempt. They'd keep him up to the wee hours of the morning, and he was late for school every day. I've got his report card to show he was late every day, and he wasn't learning anything. You can't teach a child nothing when he's up until five o'clock in the morning. . . . The mother liked to sleep all day and run the streets at night, and the daddy worked at night, too, half the time."

Walker said that when she enrolled the child in a new school, he flourished. "He started learning all kinds of things. Derek didn't even know how to skip and hop. I taught him how to walk and talk and everything. When he was at Janet's house, all he did was stay in the playpen all day."

Walker characterized Terry King as a strict, controlling father who kept Alex and Derek isolated from other children when they were young. "Terry wanted his young'uns to stay still and mind him, do every little thing he said," Walker related. "He didn't want them to play with other young'uns. He wanted to keep them isolated."

She said that he was known to yank them around, and would strike them with his hand.

"He believed in taking their pants down and whipping them real hard on their butt," Walker said. "He has whipped them and left them standing naked out in the yard."

These revelations were in stark contrast with what the boys had told the investigators, and were just the opposite of what the boys' mother, Janet, had said about Terry King.

During those occasional times when Derek would visit his mother and father, he nearly always came back upset, Walker said. On one such occasion, Derek said that his dad had threatened to kill him. When Walker had pressed him for details, Derek did not provide them. Meanwhile, according to Walker, King had become increasingly critical of her child-rearing skills.

"He said we were teaching Derek how to be a redneck," Walker said. "We were teaching him how to fish. We'd let him steer the boat a little bit. He'd go camping with us. We asked Terry what in the world was wrong with that. He said his son wasn't going to grow up to be no redneck. . . . Terry didn't want Derek to love us like he did."

She added that she did not see much of the children while they were at the Heritage Christian Academy, nor did she see much of them after they were placed in foster homes. Walker said that she believed Terry was angry with her because she and her husband had ceased giving him money, and that was his reason for not allowing her to see the children often. Janet, in the meantime, had shown little interest in the children, according to Walker.

"Janet said if they were with a good family and they got money, that was fine," Walker said.

Walker revealed an unusual family relationship: Terry King's father, Wilbur, had married Linda Walker's mother, Vesta, making her Alex and Derek's maternal grandmother, but also Terry King's stepsister. Wilbur King was married to Vesta for nineteen years, until her death in 1998. Wilbur King has since remarried.

Walker spoke of the disciplinary problems that Derek had begun having while living with the Lays. A counselor from Olive Baptist Church had called her because Derek had been asking to see her.

"She told us that Derek wanted to see us because family was real important to Derek," Walker said, "and we were the ones that Derek talked about over there."

She said that she had learned about the disciplinary problems Derek was having, but she dismissed them as being typical for his age group.

"He was just a typical teenager," Walker said. "He was getting smart-mouthed and everything. You know how a teenager is."

Walker said that Janet had called and told her he wanted to return Derek to King. Janet had asked her mother if she would take Derek instead. Walker had agreed to do so, but King would hear nothing of it.

"Terry decided that he'd rather take him than let us have him," Walker said. "Derek didn't want to go back to his daddy. He wanted to come live with us, but the Lays said they didn't have any choice but to give him back to his daddy."

Walker said that she had been curious about why King had spent a lot of time working on cars and such at Rick Chavis's mobile home in nearby Brentwood. It was apparently during that period that Chavis had taken an unsavory interest in young Alex. It was never clear to Walker or others, however, whether Terry knew about Chavis's prior record. The boys he had molested were in the same age group as Alex and Derek.

"Chavis had a lot of influence over those boys," Walker said. "That was the only attention they'd gotten, and Chavis was telling them he loved them and everything."

Meanwhile, as the case moved closer toward presentation to a grand jury, Alex and Derek's attorneys began making plans to keep the boys out of the Escambia County Jail in the likely event they would be indicted for the murder of their father. James Stokes, Alex's attorney, indicated that the boys were interacting with boys their own age at the juvenile detention center.

"These are two kids who punch and poke on each other because they are brothers," Stokes said. "I realize what they are charged with, but they are still only charged. We're very concerned about their safety in the adult jail."

If transferred to the jail, they would have to interact with adults or be kept isolated. Stokes indicated that his immediate concern was to keep them in the juvenile facility, indictment or none. Sharon Potter, Derek's attorney, agreed.

"They're babies," Potter said. "Just look at them."

CHAPTER 14

As the case moved closer to the grand jury stage, John Sanderson and Terry Kilgore, along with a host of other investigators, continued to piece together the facts. According to Escambia County Chief Deputy Larry Smith, the investigators still did not have nearly enough information to begin answering all of the questions they had. Motive was the primary mystery.

"There has to be a reason," Smith said. "We're still trying to establish the lifestyle that was going on at the household. But at this point we don't have any indication of abuse." Smith said that the detectives did not have any "direct information" that another person might be involved in King's death. "We're still trying to establish a time line for all the individuals who were known to associate with the victim."

Sanderson and Kilgore continued looking at Rick Chavis as a potential suspect in the case, but they weren't sure just how he might have been involved. Based on the conflicting stories they had received from Chavis, and numerous other sources, it appeared that he could be an accessory after the fact: He had helped the boys after their dad's death and had possibly even concealed them from the investigators before they surrendered to authorities.

Meanwhile, State Attorney Curtis Golden made the announcement that prosecutors were only a few days away from presenting their case to a grand jury. Golden said that authorities hoped to have the question of motive answered by that time.

"We're going to do all the investigating we can before next week," Golden said, indicating that the grand jury would likely hear the evidence on Tuesday, December 11, 2001. "We're going to present the case straight up and not try to influence the grand jury one way or another."

The grand jury proceeding was conducted behind closed doors at the M. C. Blanchard Building on Tuesday morning. There were a number of witnesses that filed in and out of the meeting room, including firefighters, fire investigators, sheriff's deputies, identification officers, Sanderson and Kilgore, the medical examiner and Rick Chavis. The proceeding moved along swiftly, and after all the testimony had been delivered, everyone had to wait while the grand jury mulled over all that it had heard and read.

In a move that caught a few people off guard, sheriff's deputies arrested Rick Chavis, shortly after he exited the grand jury room following his testimony. They read him his Miranda rights and whisked him off to the Escambia County Jail where he was charged with being an accessory after the fact to murder. Escambia County Sheriff Ron McNesby announced the news to the public, adding that Chavis had been accused of hiding Alex and Derek inside his Brentwood mobile home for almost two days before turning them over to sheriff's deputies. Chavis was held in lieu of $50,000 bond.

Moments later, Sheriff McNesby told a group of eager print and broadcast reporters that Alex and Derek King had been indicted by the grand jury on adult charges of first-degree premeditated murder in connection with the slaying of their father. As previously stated, a conviction on such a charge in Florida would mean an automatic mandatory life sentence without possibility of parole. The boys were promptly transferred from the juvenile detention center to the Escambia County Jail, where they would be held without bond.

"We believe that it's a very bizarre case, and it is a very sad case when you have young people like this involved," Sheriff McNesby told the group of reporters. When the reporters asked about Chavis's role in the case, McNesby took them through the circumstances of his involvement as they pertained to the charges he was facing.

McNesby recounted how Chavis had received a telephone call from a convenience store near the King home at the time the fire was burning. Investigators believed that Chavis had taken the boys to his home and had either washed their clothes for them or allowed the boys to wash their clothes with the knowledge that they had just killed their father. McNesby also revealed that the investigators had discovered that Alex and Derek had been hiding in the back bedroom of the mobile home on the day of the murder while the investigators were there asking Chavis questions.

Chavis's criminal record, according to the sheriff,

was a little more extensive than originally revealed. Although Chavis had pleaded no contest to the 1984 charges of lewd and lascivious assault on two 13-year-old boys—one of them a runaway from a drug rehabilitation center—and had been ordered to serve six months in jail and was placed on five years probation, he had also committed a burglary and petty theft in 1986. That offense had resulted in the revocation of his probation and had landed him in state prison for nine years. He was released from prison in 1989 after serving barely three years. He faced another theft charge in 1996, but the charges were dropped in that case.

That evening, after the grand jury had convened, with Chavis locked away in jail, investigators converged on his mobile home again to conduct a thorough search. As they entered the gate, bright spotlights lighting up the yard, the investigators noted Chavis's elaborate security system. The older model trailer was behind a tall wooden fence, and a numeric code was needed to open the gate without setting off the alarm. They also noted the presence of electric wire at various locations, some of which were apparently connected to surveillance cameras that had been strategically placed around the trailer and the entrance to the yard. There were also several warning and "No Trespassing" signs posted along the outside of the wooden fence, along the top of which ran three strands of electrified wire. The detectives wondered why Chavis felt he needed such elaborate security. The neighborhood was dark and somewhat isolated and perhaps, some believed, he felt it was necessary to discourage burglars. Others considered that perhaps he felt he needed it for his own personal safety.

Several of Chavis's neighbors congregated outside the gate of the mobile home as the investigators worked throughout the evening. Many of the neighbors talked to the media that was also camped outside; some said that Chavis's home was often filled with teenage boys regardless of the time—they were there day and night. Others voiced their feelings about Chavis as a neighbor.

"When I first met him, I thought he was a helpful neighbor," said a man who lived a few houses away. "In fact, he helped us quite a bit with our Neighborhood Watch program. But later I decided I would keep a little distance from him." The neighbor said that he kept his 13-year-old son away from Chavis's home because he was concerned about all of the boys who were coming and going late at night and was worried that they might be using drugs. "I didn't want my son associating with that," said the neighbor.

"He seemed all right when I would see him on the street," said another neighbor. "But I didn't want my kids over there." The neighbor said that she had allowed her two teenager kids to visit Chavis's home on only one occasion. One of her kids, a 14-year-old girl, told her that Chavis had numerous video games and that the neighborhood kids would go over there to play them. Although the neighbor said that she would not allow her children to go back to his home again, she said that she never suspected that anything illegal had been occurring there.

A few of the neighbors told reporters that they had seen Alex and Derek at Chavis's home before, but no one recalled having seen them recently.

"If those kids were there, they did a good job of

hiding them, because none of us saw them," said the neighbor, who would not allow her children to return to Chavis's home.

Another neighbor, Tony Goodale, 35, a father of six children, who lives about a block from Chavis's trailer, said that at first, "He just had a regular fence up there. The next thing we know, boom, it's a fortress."

Goodale said that two of his children had frequently visited Chavis several years earlier, when they were 10 and 11. However, when Goodale learned about Chavis's criminal record as a sex offender, he would no longer allow his children to go near Rick's home.

"That really upset me," Goodale said. "My boys said he never got out of hand with them in any way, but it upset me."

Yet another of Chavis's neighbors, Laura McLellan, a 31-year-old mother of a 2-year-old boy, did not know Chavis personally and had not heard of him until all of the media attention made him well-known throughout the community. She recognized him from photos that had appeared on the news, however, and realized that he lived near her. She expressed feelings of anger that she, like everyone else in the neighborhood, had not been informed that a convicted sex offender was living nearby.

"I always thought he led a strange life," she said. "If I'd come in late, his gate would be open and I'd see all those boys in there. He did seem strange. . . . It's very disturbing and scary to know someone like that was living down the street. I don't understand how a neighborhood isn't informed of something like that. It's unreal."

The residents had not been notified, it was pointed out, because the sex offender community notification laws were not on the books when Chavis was convicted. Those laws had not gone into effect until about five years earlier, and thus did not apply to Chavis. If he had been convicted of a sex crime after those laws had been passed law enforcement would have been required to notify the community of his presence.

Meanwhile, on Wednesday, December 12, 2001, Alex and Derek King, through their attorneys, entered written pleas of not guilty at what would have normally been their arraignment. The written pleas enabled them to avoid a public court appearance.

Rick Chavis made his first court appearance on the same morning that Alex and Derek entered their pleas. He appeared via closed circuit television, accompanied by assistant public defender Clint Davis. Chavis, in what appeared to be a claim of indigence, told Escambia County Judge David Ackerman that his only assets consisted of two older model cars and the mobile home where he lived with his brother. The mobile home, he said, was still mortgaged.

Judge Ackerman ordered that Chavis's bond remain at $50,000, and that he have no contact with either Alex or Derek. Ackerman, after reviewing the details of Chavis's assets, ordered the public defender's office to represent him.

It wasn't long before details of how Alex and Derek were doing in the adult jail began trickling out. Reverend Stan Lewis, an associate pastor at Olive

Baptist Church, was among those who provided details following a visit with the boys.

"They're doing okay," Lewis said. "They were
playing with other kids in the juvenile center. That's
changed now, of course. I think their spirits are pretty
good right now, but I don't think there's been a real
impact of what they're facing."

"The only place to keep kids in the jail," said
Alex's attorney, James Stokes, "is in the special
housing unit. That's the same place they lock up
child molesters. I'm sure the jail will take precautions. But it's just the idea of throwing twelve-year-
olds in there."

Stokes said that he and Derek's attorney, Sharon
Potter, would continue trying to convince the judge
to return the boys to the juvenile detention center
where they could receive schooling and interrelate
with children their own age.

CHAPTER 15

Immediately after receiving Alex and Derek's written not-guilty pleas from their lawyers Escambia County Circuit Judge Linda Nobles set a trial date for March 11, 2002. Because of the complexities of the case and the fact that the investigation was continuing, the trial date did not seem realistic. There was also the Rick Chavis leg of the investigation. No one at this point would even venture a guess as to how Chavis might impact the case. The only thing that was certain was that Alex and Derek would stand trial for murder, and that Prosecutor David Rimmer was adamant that any kind of plea bargain attempt would be unacceptable to him.

"In cases involving death," Rimmer said, "I don't plea-bargain. I'd rather let the jury decide. When a human life has been taken, I'd rather let the jury decide what, if anything, the defendant should be convicted of." Rimmer conceded that this case would be difficult for a jury to decide.

"There will be some severe challenges, certainly, because of the public's feelings about prosecuting somebody of this age," he continued. "We'll see if we can get jurors to judge them by their actions and not by their ages. Legally, it's not an issue. If it was, they wouldn't be in an adult courtroom."

Florida was one of fifteen states that permitted juveniles to be tried as adults at the time. Statistics showed that in 1998, the state had the most juveniles in adult prisons—578. The fairness of such laws would become an issue, at least in Florida, because of the King boys. There was already considerable talk among legislators about changing the law, much to the annoyance of Senator Victor Crist, its author.

"I wrote the law," Crist said. "I chair that committee, and it ain't changing. They know what they're doing at that point [age]. They know a gun kills. They know a bullet kills. And they know what 'dead' means. . . . That is the bottom line. We're not talking accidental manslaughter. There's a big difference there. If they're that age, and they take another man's life in cold blood, chances are they're going to do it again. They have no regard for human life. Period."

In Florida, the debate on prosecuting and sentencing juveniles as adults seemed to focus on three basic questions: 1) Do kids really know what they're doing as they are committing a crime? 2) Do children have an understanding of the consequences of their actions? 3) Are they capable of understanding the legal proceedings in the courtroom and the potential sentences that they might receive if convicted?

In the ordeal surrounding Alex and Derek King, most people, especially their relatives, respond with a resounding "No" to those three questions. One such person, the boys' step-cousin Sheila Walker, began circulating a petition for leniency for the boys which she intended to submit to the state attorney's office.

"I remember being thirteen," Walker said. "Your head is messed up even if you have a normal childhood. They're kids. They have the minds of kids."

Psychologist Ron Belter, who is also an associate professor at the University of West Florida, agrees that children of Alex's and Derek's ages do not make decisions in the same manner as an adult would.

"Our society is based on the belief that individuals who are not competent should not be held fully responsible for their actions," Belter said. "There is a reason that we do not let twelve- or thirteen-year-olds drive a vehicle, vote, drink alcohol or use tobacco products. We do not think they are old enough to make wise decisions based on their best interests. So why is it different in the case of a crime?"

Another relative of Alex and Derek suggested that the boys should be sent to a juvenile detention facility and that they should receive psychological counseling until they reached legal age, at which point it should be determined whether they are released or sentenced to prison.

"I'm elected by the people, and I am the chief law enforcement officer of my circuit," said State Attorney Harry Shortstein of Jacksonville. Shortstein opposes the laws governing juveniles as currently written. "The circuit judge is also elected by the people to do his job. We should be making the decisions, and under no circumstances should it be the legislature. Unfortunately that's what it is now. You have a tremendously qualified state attorney in Curtis Golden over there, and why should a member of the

legislature be better equipped to make the prosecutorial decisions in these cases? I wish there was a
system that could handle these younger criminals.
But in Florida, we feel that doesn't exist."

"In some cases," said State Attorney Curtis
Golden, "if they're old enough to commit an adult
crime, then they're old enough to be prosecuted as
an adult. I do feel that juveniles who commit first-
degree murder—many of those are incapable of rehabilitation and should be removed from society
forever. But again, there are juveniles who can be
rehabilitated, and they should be given every opportunity to return to society." Golden's comments
seemed like a politician wavering, unable or unwill-
ing to take a firm stand on the issue.

Although David Rimmer had received numerous
complaints from the public about prosecuting Alex
and Derek as adults, he expressed confidence that he
could handle the job.

"I don't make the law," he said. "I just enforce it.
If the legislature did not want twelve- and thirteen-
year-olds tried as adults, it could change the law."

Rimmer felt that his biggest challenge would be
selecting a jury that could handle such a case.

"I'm just hoping that when the panel of prospec-
tive jurors is in," Rimmer said, "we will be able to
pick a jury that can be fair and impartial and won't
be influenced by feelings of sympathy and bias because of their ages."

As Christmas approached, it became more obvious
that Alex and Derek would spend the Yuletide season
behind bars in the Escambia County Jail. The boys'
attorneys had been unsuccessful in finding legal
grounds that would convince a judge to return the

children to the juvenile detention center. Nonetheless, Alex's attorney, James Stokes, said that the boys were being treated particularly well in the jail. They had been isolated from the other inmates, and Chavis was being held four floors beneath them. They were allowed to watch television, make phone calls and read, and they were being tutored. They also had exercise privileges outdoors at a time when other inmates were not allowed outside.

All-in-all, the attorneys reasoned, it could have been worse.

Right after Christmas, on Friday, December 28, the attorneys for the children went before a judge and sought their clients' release on bond. They argued in their motion that both boys had relatives living in the area and were not flight risks. Alex and Derek were present in the courtroom wearing drab green jail-issued jumpsuits. They were handcuffed and their ankles were shackled. They sat quietly throughout most of the hearing, with Alex barely able to see over the rail in front of him. When the well-groomed boys weren't smiling at relatives and others they knew in the courtroom, they messed around with their handcuffs and fidgeted in their seats.

Under oath, Alex and Derek were asked brief questions relating to their status of indigence that required only yes or no responses. They had no income or assets such as real property or stocks and bonds, and could not pay for their defense, their lawyers told the judge.

At one point Prosecutor David Rimmer presented a poster that depicted crime-scene photos, some of which showed their dead father. The boys did not display any emotion. Similarly, when Detective John

Sanderson testified about the contents of the boys' confessions and provided a transcript of those confessions to the judge, the boys just sat quietly. They could have easily been there observing someone else's criminal proceedings, and not their own.

At the conclusion of the 11 A.M. hearing, Escambia County Circuit Judge Kim Skievaski ruled that the boys were partially indigent and ordered the county to pay the defense team limited investigative costs at taxpayer expense. He also ruled that the county would pay for subpoena and deposition costs. The judge, however, ruled against the motions to release the children and ordered that they be held without bond.

CHAPTER 16

As the investigation continued from a number of angles, Sanderson and Kilgore kept returning to the Rick Chavis aspect. The detectives now believed that Chavis had lied, and had attempted to mislead them during his initial interviews with them. He first told them that he had not known where Alex and Derek were until the day after King's death. Then he said that he had received the telephone call from an unknown woman that led him to the boys. Then, during yet another interview with the detectives, Chavis told them that the brothers had called him from a pay phone shortly after the slaying and asked him to come and pick them up. The latter version appeared to be the truth because Sanderson had obtained Chavis's telephone records, and those records had shown that a call had been placed to his home at 1:39 A.M. on November 26 from a convenience store across the street from King's home. That call had been placed at the same time that the fire department was attempting to put out the blaze. While they were driving to his trailer after he had picked them up, he said that the boys had told him they had killed their father and had started a blaze in one of the bedrooms. When they got back to Chavis's trailer, Chavis said, he'd washed the clothes that Alex and Derek were wearing when they'd killed their dad, and allowed them to clean up.

It was during that third interview that Chavis had told them that he had allowed the boys to stay at his house the first time they ran away from home on November 16, 2001. He said that he had not told their father they were at his house, and had even assisted in King's search for his sons. He even lied to King when he came to Chavis's home looking for the boys—they were hiding in one of the trailer's bedrooms.

During the search of Chavis's home, investigators had seized twenty-two items, including a wooden pipe that was used to smoke marijuana, drug paraphernalia, marijuana seeds, computer hardware and software, articles of boys' clothing and a broken, red aluminum baseball bat that had been recovered from the back yard.

It was soon determined that the bat was not the one used to kill King. Investigators believed that bat, or what was left of it, had been found inside King's house, little more than a molten chunk of metal. Tests were being conducted to try to determine whether they were right.

"In their statements they said they threw the bat on the bed," said Prosecutor David Rimmer. "But since no bat was discovered it caused some concerns."

Alex's attorney, James Stokes, believed that the melted metal was all that was left of the bat. According to Stokes, the recovery of the murder weapon would not have any impact on his defense of Alex.

"We don't even know who put the bat there," Stokes said. "Right now I'm beginning to wonder who swung the bat."

"I'm not surprised that he [Stokes] is going to argue that," Rimmer said. "But we certainly don't have any evidence of that. Basically the boys were not happy with their dad. He was too strict with them, and they wanted to be with Rick Chavis. They ran away, and when that didn't work, they killed him."

On Friday, January 4, 2002, Rick Chavis pleaded innocent to being an accessory after the fact of murder. Circuit Judge Linda Nobles immediately set a trial date for March 25. As with Alex and Derek's scheduled court appearance, the date did not appear realistic and would likely be pushed back.

In an interview Chavis had with Sanderson and Kilgore, Chavis said he'd promised Alex and Derek that they could come and live with him in the event that their father died. The promise had been made only hours before Terry's murder. During the interview, Chavis repeatedly denied that he had urged the boys to kill their father. He also denied any involvement in helping the boys plan their father's demise, and denied any foreknowledge of their plans.

"If I had prior knowledge that Terry was gonna get killed, I would have stopped it," Chavis told the cops.

When asked about the so-called "love" relationship between himself and Alex, Chavis admitted that he had told the boys that he loved them and they likewise had told him that they loved him. But he insisted that their professions of love were never inappropriate. He said that Alex knew that Chavis was gay, but that when Alex had indicated his feelings for Chavis they were not "out of the father–son type relationship." He insisted that Alex had "never pushed it to a point of making me think that he was after some kind of relationship with me. . . . I'm not sexually active. I've been out of it now, eight, nine years or better."

On the day that Chavis returned Alex to his father, and only hours prior to the killing, the boys told him that they did not plan to stay with Terry, Chavis told investigators.

"I told them, well, if they left again to give me a call and I'd come pick them up," Chavis said.

At one point Chavis described the early morning phone call that he had received from Alex and Derek from the convenience store.

"I heard Derek say, 'Hurry up and come get us,' and I heard Alex babbling," Chavis said. "I flew up there. . . . Alex was in shock," he said. "And Derek was real upset." He said the boys climbed in his car and told him what had happened. He said that he also told Alex and Derek not to tell the police investigators that he had concealed them from their father and the cops. The following day, while he was still harboring them, the boys had told him once again that they wanted to live with him, he said.

"Even after everything that's happened," said one of the investigators, "you still want them boys to come live with you, don't you?"

"Yes," Chavis replied. "It's the truth."

At about the same time that the transcripts of Chavis's interviews with the detectives were released, additional documents were made public that shed a little more light on Derek, his state of mind in the weeks leading up to the killing and the problems that prompted Frank and Nancy Lay to send him back to his father. Nothing that was released, however, gave much indication that Alex and Derek had been subjected to any serious physical abuse, despite the allegations made by their maternal grandmother.

Although the Lays have steadfastly declined to speak publicly about the case or their relationship with Derek, interviews between the Lays and a Florida Department of Children and Families investigator provided a few more details regarding their reasons for returning Derek to Terry.

Although Derek had not done anything violent while at the Lays', his behavior had continuously deteriorated in the weeks leading up to their decision to restore custody to his father. Frank Lay had told the investigator that Derek was an intelligent and a very personable boy, but that he had begun stealing things, purchasing pornography at school, and bringing girls to their home. Lay said that Derek had also been caught with cigarettes and matches, and that his grades were falling considerably. He had also begun showing interest in drugs, and had purportedly sniffed lighter fluid in an attempt to get high. Similarly, Nancy Lay had told the investigator that Derek had started lying and stealing, and that he showed no remorse after being caught. She described him as being extremely manipulative, and characterized him as having "holes in his conscience." A few weeks before being returned to his father, he had threatened to kill himself, the Lays said. They had discovered a package of single-edge razor blades beneath his bed, and he had been observed with a number of red scratches

or cuts on his upper legs. It was not immediately
known whether those scratches or cuts had been self-
inflicted. He had also used the razor blades to slice
up his mattress. Going back a little further, Derek had
attempted to cut off the blood flow to his brain by
placing his hands around his neck, as if trying to
choke himself. Those attempts had left bruises on his
neck.

When she described Terry King to the investigator,
Nancy Lay had characterized him as "very strange,"
and said that he usually spoke in monotones. His eyes
were frequently glazed over when he would come to
visit Derek, and she presumed that he had been taking drugs. It should be pointed out that toxicology
tests conducted as part of King's autopsy had failed
to show any presence of drugs or alcohol.

By early February 2002, Alex's attorney, James
Stokes, indicated that his defense of Alex would focus on Rick Chavis. While he would not elaborate at
this stage, Stokes said that there were indications that
Chavis had been at Terry King's house on the night
of his death, although prior to the slaying. It soon
came out that Chavis had told investigators that he
had driven by King's home that evening. Stokes also
said that he believed that there was much more to
the alleged sexual involvement between the boys and
Chavis than what had been revealed.

"We are getting stuff from concerned citizens that
indicates much stronger sexual involvement than
what was alleged, and much more manipulation,"
Stokes said.

He also said he was tired of the characterizations

that people in the media were giving to Alex's and Derek's statements to the investigators. "I wish people would quit calling these *confessions*," Stokes said. "It doesn't take you two days to put together confessions. It takes you two days to put together a story."

Stokes believed the investigation may have been tainted. He said that Deputy Reggie Jernigan was a close friend of Chavis's, and shouldn't have been present during portions of Alex's and Derek's interviews with Sanderson and Kilgore. Stokes said he felt that the boys might not have been as forthcoming or truthful with the investigators because of Jernigan's presence during the interviews.

"The defense can either accept the investigation as completed by the state attorney and sheriff's office to include Reggie Jernigan, or we can continue our investigation with the assistance of the public and uncover what really happened to Terry King," Stokes said.

The Escambia County Sheriff's Office began an internal investigation into Jernigan and Chavis's relationship. According to Chief Deputy Larry Smith, such an investigation typically takes about two weeks to complete.

Stokes also said that he believed that Rick Chavis was Alex King's "adult lover." Although Chavis denied that he'd had any sexual encounters with Alex, Stokes suggested that perhaps Chavis's influence over Alex had prevented the boy from being as forthcoming as he could have been. Stokes also pleaded for the public to help by continuing to provide information.

"In cases where there is the possibility of sexual

and emotional manipulations," Stokes said, "the perpetrators and defendants often develop a bond of si-
lence that can only be broken with the aid of
information from local citizens. The defense hopes
that continued media coverage of facts already made
public will promote the flow of information from
concerned citizens to the defense."

Chavis's lawyer, Michael Rollo, promptly complained about Stokes's actions and accused him of
attempting to deflect blame away from the two brothers and toward his client. He dismissed Stokes's comments as "gossip, rumor, innuendo, speculation,
distortions, exaggerations, pulp fiction, silly argument and deliberately ignorant assertions."

Stokes retorted that it should not be surprising if
his efforts at defending Alex involved Chavis. "The
statement that the defense will be focusing on the role
of Rick Chavis, although offensive to Mr. Chavis, is
as obvious as the fact that spring follows winter,"
Stokes said. Stokes reiterated that the defense was
following as many leads as possible, including following up on details revealed during press coverage
such as a *Dateline NBC* report that had aired on national television. *Dateline* and other programs had
presented information showing a part of Chavis's relationship with the King family and included interviews with Chavis and others.

"Some of these contacts," Stokes said, "indicate
that persons other than Mr. Chavis may have been
involved. The defense has a clear need to seek and
maintain public information."

Rollo promptly asked Circuit Judge Kim Skievaski
to impose a gag order on Stokes. Rollo stated that
Stokes's comments were prejudicial to Chavis, that a

number of his pleadings had been inflammatory and
fictitious, and that some of Stokes's pleadings had
been written "in the spirit of P. T. Barnum or Mark
Twain." Rollo accused Stokes of "manipulating the
public through the back door."

Stokes and Sharon Potter, Derek's attorney, as
well as Prosecutor David Rimmer, each told the
judge that they had no objection to a gag order. As
a result, Judge Skievaski ordered that none of the
attorneys speak with reporters about the case, their
trial strategies or what the evidence might indicate.
Skievaski did not, however, issue an order sealing the
attorneys' motions or other court documents.

Meanwhile, Father Val J. Peter, the leader of the
Girls and Boys Town in Nebraska, sent an "Open
Letter to the People of Pensacola," in which he compared Alex and Derek's situation to that of a much-
publicized 1937 case involving a Denver teenager
who had killed his father. In that case the prosecutor
had sought the death penalty for Billy Meagher, but
the leader of what was then known only as Boys
Town, Father Edward Flanagan, intervened and
helped arrange for Meagher to serve his sentence under his jurisdiction.

"The choice between adult court and juvenile court
is the wrong focus," Peter wrote in his open letter.
"The debate should be about how these boys were
. . . convinced to do what they did and what factors
helped them to be convinced." Peter stated that children who are of the ages of Alex and Derek possess
a different concept of truth than adults, and can be
easily manipulated by adults. He also pointed out that

children generally do not possess the impulse control that adults do.

"I stand in Father Flanagan's shoes," Peter wrote, "and like him, I have dealt with these children for decades. It is never as simple as it appears."

On February 21, one of the corrections officers at the Escambia County Jail observed Alex kicking his cell door and running into it in what appeared to be an attempt to injure himself. Alex sustained bruises to both of his arms as a result of the incident. When he was examined in the infirmary, officials discovered a three-inch cut on one of his forearms. Alex said that he had inflicted that injury with a mechanical pencil. Only a few hours earlier the same jailer had heard Derek saying that he wanted to electrocute himself. As a result of Derek's comments and Alex's actions, the boys were separated. Alex was removed from the cell that he had shared with Derek and was placed in the cell next door.

"They were medically evaluated both for their physical and mental well-being," said Dennis Williams, jail director. "We don't feel that either one of them is in any danger."

It was also reported that, a few days earlier, Chavis had been seen by a jail guard using a small rock to scratch something into the cement of the jail's recreation yard. He was unable to finish the message before guards interrupted him. However, they noted that he had written, "Alex don't trust," causing everyone to wonder what name he had been planning to scratch into the cement. The message was obliterated prior to Alex and Derek being let back into the yard.

CHAPTER 17

The next move was not particularly unexpected. On Friday, March 22, Escambia County Sheriff Ron McNesby announced to the public that the internal affairs investigation into the relationship between Deputy Reggie Jernigan and Rick Chavis had been completed. Based on the results, McNesby said that he had made the decision to fire Jernigan because he had violated regulations against associating with criminals and engaging in conduct that was deemed unbecoming of an officer.

"His close personal friendship with Ricky Chavis is unacceptable and has caused extreme embarrassment to the community, his fellow officers and to this agency," McNesby said. Jernigan, he said, had been employed in law enforcement for twenty-three years.

It was revealed that Jernigan had been a jailer when he met Chavis in the early 1980s when Chavis was an inmate at the jail. The investigation turned up evidence that Jernigan visited Chavis frequently at his home. Neighbors told detectives that they had seen Jernigan's patrol car parked outside Chavis's trailer on many occasions.

Jernigan, when questioned by investigators, said that Chavis sometimes repaired his car, and that they also socialized. Often, when Jernigan visited Chavis, there were teenagers and young adults present playing video games on Chavis's PlayStation while others worked on repairing their bicycles. Jernigan said that he had seen Alex King at Chavis's home on at least ten to fifteen occasions and that he had seen Derek there on approximately five occasions. Jernigan said that although he suspected that Chavis smoked marijuana, he never witnessed him doing anything illegal.

Jernigan made it clear that he would take legal action and appeal his dismissal.

Despite the court order barring Rick Chavis from having any contact with the King brothers, officials found another message that appeared to be from him on March 26. Unlike the one he attempted to scratch into the cement of the recreation yard, this message had been written on the wall of a courthouse holding cell that Chavis had occupied six days earlier. Although they could not prove that Chavis was the author of the message, he was at the top of their suspect list. The message had been left unsigned, but it included Alex's and Derek's names. It read, in part: "Hang in there. It will work out if nothing changes in the testimony. You know who not to trust. They are just keeping us apart until this is over."

Chavis denied that he had written the message.

On Saturday, April 6, while Alex was outside in

the jail yard playing, one of the jailers entered his cell to empty his trash can. As he did so, he found two crumpled-up pieces of paper. When he opened them up, he discovered that one of them appeared to be a note from Chavis to Alex. The note read:

I'm always thinking about ya. Hang in there it will work out if nothing changes in the testemony. You know who not to trust, they are keeping us apart until this is over. [Just say NO] [Drawn symbol deleted] Always and forever. I think about you day and night. Please be careful. I'm with you and your thoughts. Our future depend on the outcome of us in court and what happen to us. Just be strong and please don't change anything. And hang in there, you know what your lawyer did to me. And that is not your fault but he is trying to break you down— don't give in. If a deal has been promise to get you to say yes about certain things . . . [Illegible] Be bold and be strong nothing has changed. I'm still here and watch who you trust everything going alright so far. They want me bad you all heard what was said and who said those things about me and now be smart and sit back and listen. I'll still be waiting don't forget my address and phone number. Whatever happen try to stay in touch with me or Mike, he is watching the house right now. We will be kept a part they are trying to make you'll talk and get me 50 years in prison. Remember what we talk about they will try to make you believe that they already know and they really don't. It's a mind game. Don't be played and don't change nothing even under oath only . . . [Illegible] They will not keep there promises. They will lie to you to get you to talk please

don't give in I'm still with you. I L U always and
forever you know who. [Drawn symbol deleted] Alex
Derek King Always [Drawn symbol deleted] For-
ever. I L U forever. Be strong and be patient. I'm
still with you. Watch who you talk to. I will always
be here for you, nothing changed, everything is still
the same, even in court.

Because of the special efforts and precautions being taken by the jail staff to keep Chavis away from
Alex and Derek, it was a mystery how the note made
it into the cell. Since no one was talking, it was likely
a mystery that would never be solved.

On yet another occasion, during a visit between
the King boys and their maternal grandfather, Jimmie
Wayne French, a jailer overheard part of a loud conversation between them. Derek had asked his grandfather whether he had heard from Chavis. French told
the boy that he hadn't spoken to Chavis for several
weeks, but that he expected to hear from him soon,
within a week or so. For reasons that weren't entirely
clear, Alex turned around and faced the guard who
was listening, perhaps to discourage him from listening and to move along, and asked him, "How are you
doing?"

In another instance, a routine check for contraband
turned up what appeared to be a makeshift weapon
in Derek's cell. The supposed weapon consisted of a
broken pencil in which the lead had been removed,
leaving it hollow in the center. Into the hollowed-out
pencil a paperclip had been inserted far enough that
it protruded from one end, and the other end had
been bent over to keep it from slipping all the way
through. The result was a semi-sharp instrument that

could easily be concealed in a person's hand, capable of inflicting damage to another person. Whatever it was that Derek had planned to do with the potential weapon was yet another mystery.

After spending nearly five months in jail, Alex and Derek's court date was pushed back to August 26, 2002, following a court hearing in February 2002. Two months later, in April, another grand jury was convened, this time, apparently, for hearing evidence against Chavis and to consider his possible involvement in Terry King's death. It wasn't immediately clear if this was instigated by the note Alex had received. Whatever the reason, Alex and Derek King were called to testify behind the closed-door secret proceedings. At their conclusion on Wednesday, April 10, it was announced that Rick Chavis had been indicted on charges of first-degree, premeditated murder in the death of Terry King. Chavis had also been indicted on charges of arson and lewd and lascivious sexual battery of a child 12 or older, and tampering with evidence.

It should be recalled that in their original statements to Investigators Sanderson and Kilgore, the boys had said that it was Alex's idea to kill his father and that Derek had actually carried out the murder. They also told the cops that Rick Chavis did not have prior knowledge of the slaying. That a grand jury had indicted Chavis shortly after hearing testimony from the boys could only mean one thing—they had changed their story.

As the questions began to pour into the prosecutor's office over the new revelations, Assistant State Attorney David Rimmer said that Chavis's indictment did not change anything with regard to Alex and Derek King's charges. The original charges against the boys would remain, and now there would be a new defendant who would be tried separately from the boys. Rimmer said that he would not pursue the death penalty against Chavis. He also stated that Chavis's indictment might serve to weaken the prosecution's case against the King boys.

"It all depends on how jurors perceive that," Rimmer said. Rimmer allowed the possibility of a plea bargain with Chavis, in which Chavis would be required to testify against the two boys. That would necessitate significant discussion, however, between himself and Chavis's attorney. Because of the gag order, Rimmer was not permitted to comment further about the case or the charges against Chavis.

At his arraignment on Thursday, May 2, Chavis pleaded innocent to the latest round of charges. Chavis's lawyer entered his client's plea before Circuit Judge Michael Jones, who initially set a trial date for October 21.

As August approached and it appeared that no plea bargain with Chavis was forthcoming, it was mutually agreed upon by all parties that Chavis would be tried first for the murder of Terry King, as well as on arson charges. Chavis's trial date was changed to Monday, August 26, 2002. The other charges facing Chavis would be dealt with later, depending upon the outcome of his murder trial. If he were found guilty of murder and arson, the possibility, even likelihood, existed that the additional charges would be dropped. If found innocent, on the other hand, prosecutors could still go after him on the other counts of accessory after the fact, tampering with evidence and lewd and lascivious sexual battery of a child 12 or older. Convictions on any of those charges, given his prior criminal record, would result in significant prison time.

In the days leading up to his trial, Chavis received considerable press coverage, both local and national. During his many interviews with the press, since he wasn't a party to the gag orders, Chavis took the opportunity to tell the community and the nation that he was incapable of hurting anyone.

"My big problem," Chavis said in an interview with a reporter from the *Pensacola News Journal*, "is that I like to help people." When questioned about his possible involvement in King's death, Chavis denied any involvement other than helping the boys after the fact.

"It ain't true that I was there," Chavis said. "That's a setup. That's all I can tell you. They were coached into it. . . . They're children, and most adults are weak to children. But that will have to be seen when the time comes." Chavis said that he was concerned that a jury might believe the boys.

During his interviews, Chavis admitted that he had lied to the investigators initially about helping Derek and Alex because he did not want to be incarcerated again. He said that he had promised his mother prior to her death in 1994 that he would never go back to prison. "For being an accessory," he said, "I knew I'd be locked up again."

Chavis said he only helped the boys because he cared very much for them and only wanted to help them when they called him after killing their father.

"I had no prior knowledge of the murder at all," Chavis said. "All I know is they called me after they done it."

Although he had been critical of his former friend, Terry King, in the past, he had no ill will toward him and had never wished any harm to come to him.

"It took me a while to get over his death," Chavis said. "I still have the pain from it. Even though I had problems with Terry, I still considered him a friend. I just gave him a washing machine and delivered it to his house before he died."

Chavis denied the allegations that he had sexually abused Alex.

"I didn't have any kind of special relationship with Alex," he said. "I care about both boys. But I care about all children."

Before his trial Chavis talked extensively with one James Isom, an inmate in the next cell. What Chavis didn't know is that Isom was also talking to prosecutor David Rimmer. In addition to conversing frequently, Chavis and Isom passed notes back and forth.

In one communication from Isom to Rimmer, Isom wrote that Chavis was not "too far from losing it. . . . He paces 22 hours a day and sleeps little. He is on the verge of going off the deep end."

A note that Chavis wrote to Isom said that the boys were his "Number 1 concern," and that he would, if possible, find a way around the court order that had barred him from having contact with Alex and Derek.

"I am somehow going to establish some kind of communication with the boys so I could help keep them straight on everything," Chavis wrote in one note. He also wrote of possibly trying to contact friends who might be willing to write to Alex and Derek and pass along what he had to say. It was never determined whether Chavis had accomplished that task.

In another note, Chavis wrote of having seen Alex walking past his cell with a group of other juveniles. At that time, according to Chavis, he and Alex had used sign language, which he had taught the boy.

"I'm glad that Alex knows sign language because I was able to tell him not to trust anyone that is trying to turn us against each other," Chavis wrote. He also wrote: "And I love the both of them. And he [Alex] said [through sign language], 'I want and I love you' before he got out of view."

Jail officials, however, do not believe that that encounter actually happened, because of the tight security in place to keep Chavis and the boys apart from each other.

Throughout the correspondence between Chavis and Isom, Chavis never once admitted to being at the crime scene, nor did he admit that he ever encouraged the boys to harm their father.

"I had no knowledge of the killing until about an hour or so after I picked the boys up," Chavis wrote. He also never mentioned seeing the fire at King's house, even though he claims he picked up the boys from a convenience store across the street.

"I did not take the boys right in [to the sheriff's department] because Alex was in a bad state of shock and it took a day to calm him down," Chavis wrote in another note to Isom. "I could not see turning the boys over to the investigators in a bad state of shock and getting pounded with questions. I just could not let that happen. They are well-mannered boys, especially the younger one."

Chavis wrote that although he had washed the boys' clothes after bringing them to his home after the murder, he was not attempting to tamper with the evidence or to get rid of bloodstains.

"They wanted to take a shower," Chavis wrote, "and neither one of them had any blood on them except two small spots on Derek's face and I had a full load of clothes after they took a shower, so I turned on the washer. I did not think that washing their clothes would be a problem."

In yet other notes to Isom, Chavis wrote that he did not molest Alex, stating that he would never hurt a child. "I did not do anything with the boys sexually," he wrote, "because first I would try to hurt anyone that tries anything with any child. And besides I'm against child molestation."

Apparently a visitor had told Chavis about the diary in which Alex wrote how Rick Chavis had made him gay, and that he wanted to grow up to be like him.

"I never knew about that," Chavis wrote to Isom. "And if I did, I would have told him that he would have to wait at least until 16 or 18 years of age and discover on his own what he wants in life because I cannot show him . . . I am not sexually active because I had a bad relationship seven years ago, and I decided not to get sexually involved with anyone at all. That would explain about the sex issue."

Chavis wrote that he was worried that Alex and Derek may have killed their father so that they could live with him. He said that he hoped that was not the motive for the killing. He claimed that he did not want to have to testify against the boys, and that he would plead the Fifth Amendment if possible. Chavis also told Isom how his own father had ignored him when he was growing up, and that he never wanted that to happen to Alex.

"I don't want Alex living the same hell I had to because he still has a future and mine is pretty well screwed," Chavis wrote. "And I will do anything to protect that future for Alex. Do you understand what I mean?"

If convicted of the murder charges, Chavis would receive a mandatory life sentence with no parole. If convicted of arson he would get another 30 years. If convicted of the lewd and lascivious act upon a child under 16 years old he would likely be sentenced to 15 years. If convicted of being an accessory after the fact of murder, his possible sentence could be 30 years, and an additional 5 years could be added if convicted on the tampering with evidence charge.

CHAPTER 18

Rick Chavis's life had always been a mess of sorts. Even he had said as much. Despite his prior criminal record and the fact that he's a convicted child molester who has been labeled a pedophile, there are people who have characterized him as a likeable person. Jan Mayhall, 37, met Chavis through Deputy Reggie Jernigan—who also happened to be her landlord—and considered him a friend, the *Pensacola News Journal* reported. Mayhall, who no longer lives in Florida, never even considered Chavis's criminal record, primarily because she met him through a law enforcement officer.

"Rick is just your average guy," Mayhall said. "We didn't know he was gay for a year. He's just a good ol' boy . . . I knew he had committed burglaries and done jail time, but that was years and years ago." She said that she had not known about his child molestation charges until recently, but that wouldn't have caused her to think any differently about him, because of all the time that had passed since the crime had been committed.

"He's a helpful person," Mayhall added. "Rick can fix anything. He can look at it and fix it. He's one of those jack of all trades, master of none."

She said that he once sold her son a car, and also worked on her car. If she did not have money to pay him for some service, he would do the work for food. She said that Chavis had never appeared violent, and she sincerely believed that he would never have suggested killing anyone. Mayhall said that Chavis told her that he was guilty of the accessory after the fact and evidence tampering charges, but she understood why he did what he did.

"He said Alex was just devastated," Mayhall said. "He said Derek was just kind of quiet and laid-back, but Alex was in hysterics . . . Rick's a caring person. If he had called the police right away, that probably would have devastated the boys even more. He shouldn't have done it, but he did."

Steve Bell, 24, a friend and ex-lover, also characterized Chavis as likeable, the *Pensacola News Journal* reported. Bell, who resided in a trailer park in West Pensacola, was 15 and a runaway when he and Chavis moved to New Orleans and began a sexual relationship with each other. Bell, who told a reporter that his father-in-law is Chavis's childhood foster brother, later married and had a child. He said that the sexual relationship he had with Chavis had been instigated by him and not Chavis.

"He told me, 'No, I can get in trouble for this, maybe when you are older,'" Bell said. "I just kept pushing him and pushing him and telling him no, that's what I wanted. It was something he was really uncomfortable with." Bell, said he did not believe that Chavis molested Alex or attempted a sexual relationship. "I told him straight up, 'If you have a relationship with this boy, it's going to get you in trouble.' I said, 'Don't do it.' He said, 'I'm not. I'm going to wait until he's older.'"

"I almost feel like he [Alex] was in the position I was in, looking for a way out of the house," Bell said. "It don't even look like a true-to-believe relationship. It looked like, 'If I make Rick believe I want to have a relationship with him, I'll get out of the house and won't even have to live with my dad.'"

Bell said that he did not believe that Chavis had anything to do with Terry King's death, nor did he believe that Chavis would have suggested that the King boys kill their father.

"When me and my brother ran away, Rick never said, 'Now look, you need to kill your dad or you need to kill your mom to avoid the problem,'" Bell said. "Rick told us we needed to go back home, tried to talk us into going back home."

Bell, however, told Chavis that he wanted to leave town rather than return to his parents'. That was when they hatched the plan to move to New Orleans.

"Rick said, 'That ain't a good idea,'" Bell said. "'If you're gonna go, somebody needs to be with you and make sure nothing happens to you.'"

Bell said that he and Chavis had lived together in New Orleans for approximately six months, then returned to Pensacola when Chavis's grandmother died. They lived together in Pensacola for about four years. Bell, who left school when he was a sixth-grader, said that Chavis assisted him with reading, encouraged him to go back to school and taught him how to repair cars. Bell said that he was grateful to Chavis for not deserting him when he was on the streets.

"He's been there for me when no one else has been," Bell said.

Public records, however, depicted a different story. According to court documents, Bell filed a domestic violence injunction against Chavis in 1998 after he'd talked to a woman on the phone. He said the telephone conversation had angered Chavis and, in a jealous rage, the older man "slammed" him against the bed and proceeded to verbally abuse him. Years earlier, Bell wrote in his court statement, Chavis had thrown him to the floor in another jealous rage.

"There was a lot of violence in the past," Bell wrote in the court papers. "He is a very jealous man. If he sees me with anyone, he will threaten me."

Although a temporary or restraining order was issued against Chavis, it was dismissed when Bell failed to show up for the hearing.

"Ricky kind of got mad at me," Bell said. "But I think I may have overstated it a bit. I was younger and, like anybody, I didn't want to take no chances."

As the cases moved toward trial, more information began to leak out. Among the things revealed was that Chavis, at one point, had told sheriff's investigators that Derek and Alex had killed their father. Similarly, when Alex and Derek had provided their deposition before a closed-door grand jury on April 9, they had said that it had been Chavis who had swung the bat and killed their father. The boys, in their deposition, said that they had been outside the house at the time. They said that Chavis had told them about what had happened later.

At another point it was revealed that Escambia County Jail inmate Robert Smith, 21, had provided investigators with information indicating that Chavis knew about King's impending murder before it occurred.

"He was just telling us mainly that he knew that death was going to happen to Terry King, but it was just a matter of time," Smith said.

Another inmate, Allen Kozelka, told the cops that Chavis was involved in the slaying to a much larger degree than what had been believed initially. He also said that Chavis had admitted that he'd had a sexual relationship with Alex, including one sexual encounter on the night of the murder.

"He's told me that he has had an affair with Alex," Kozelka said. "And it's quite severe. He said he is in love with the boy."

Like Smith, Kozelka told the investigators that Chavis was at the crime scene the night of King's death.

"He was there, at the house," Kozelka said. "And he also went back around to check at the house. And he checked with a deputy who was there at the scene that told him that Terry was in fact killed."

On the other hand, while Alex and Derek were incarcerated at the juvenile detention center before being moved to the Escambia County Jail, several of the juvenile inmates there told the investigators that the brothers had steadfastly maintained their original story to the investigators—that they had killed their father, with Derek swinging the bat. One boy told the detectives that a violent reaction by their father that evening had been the straw that broke the camel's back. "Their dad had been, like, yelling at them and stuff and had grabbed Alex and slung him into the television," the boy said.

Another juvenile inmate said that, when he had asked Alex and Derek why they were in the detention center, they laughed and told him they were there because they had stolen some things. Later, the boy said, they changed their story. "The oldest brother," said the boy, "thought it was okay and he grabbed hold of a baseball bat and . . . killed his dad. Kept on hitting him in the face."

Yet another juvenile inmate said that he did not believe the boys at first because of how young they were. "Then he [Alex] said that they hit him in the head with a bat and burned down the house and ran away," the juvenile said.

In the final analysis, no one knew for sure who did what, and it boiled down to whether a jury would believe Rick Chavis, a convicted child molester, or the two young boys with angelic faces.

"If you're removed from this, and you don't know anyone, this is a John Grisham novel," said Reverend Ted Traylor as Chavis's trial date drew nearer. "It's got all of the pieces. But when you get up close and you know someone, you've got a different slant. If you know their momma or you know them, it gets close to your heart. This has not just drama, it has personal impact on a lot of people. Somebody's going to make a choice, a decision, a judgment. And then we'll be able to move on to the next chapter and help these boys with whatever's going to happen in their life. . . . This won't be the end of anything. It will be the opening of a new life for these boys. This is going to be a completely new chapter of their life, no matter what they walk into, whether it's prison or juvenile detention, or whether they walk free."

As the boys awaited their fate, Derek was placed on a disciplinary restraint in early August, where he remained as the trials approached. He was unable to have visitors and could not make any phone calls. Jail officials would not comment on the reason for the disciplinary action. Lisa French, the boys' paternal step-grandmother, who had visited them frequently, told reporters that they were holding up reasonably well under the circumstances.

"Alex is still pretty cheerful," French said. "But he's got cabin fever. He seems brain-dead. He doesn't display his emotions or opinions. You have to dig for it. But you can tell they're sick of it [jail]."

They seemed particularly tired of being called "dad killer" by other jail inmates who taunted them at times.

Jimmy Walker, the boys' maternal step-grandfather, told reporters that he and the boys' grandmother would make every attempt to obtain custody of Alex and Derek if they were acquitted.

"That's been their wish all along," Walker said. "And that's what we want. None of this would have ever happened if they would have been with us from the start. . . . We just want it to be over with. Everybody does. We just pray to God they're found innocent, which we think they are, and in our hearts we know they are."

Several outspoken critics, including the boys' relatives and some complete strangers, opposed the boys being charged as adults and tried in adult court. State Attorney Curtis Golden's office received phone calls as well as letters and e-mails asking the state to drop the adult charges, but Golden steadfastly maintained that the boys would be tried as adults. One group, the Community of Sant'Egidio out of Italy, urged that a mass e-mail campaign be directed at Golden's office, an effort that was in part instigated by Brian Oliver, 32, a convicted child abuser from Missouri. Oliver, who served six years in prison for sexually abusing young boys, has persistently sought to have the adult charges dropped.

"Despite the law, the fact is, children are not as mature as grown-ups regardless of their actions," Oliver told the news media. "God did not design them to handle the loads that are placed on their shoulders in the same way grown-ups handle them. . . . I've been out for three years. I've been through multiple treatment programs. It's my past. Right now, I'm living for God. I don't have time for anything else."

Oliver, citing his own prison experience, told reporters that he did not believe that Alex and Derek would be safe in an adult correctional institution.

Reverend Thomas Masters, who was pastor to Nathaniel Brazill, the boy who shot teacher Barry Grunow and was found guilty of second-degree murder and sentenced to 28 years in prison, publicly announced that he would be coming to Pensacola to become involved in the King case. Masters has previously testified before a United Nations commission in Geneva, Switzerland, that the U.S. routinely violates the human rights of children by trying them as adults and sentencing them to long terms in prison.

"I'm coming basically to monitor the case and to give moral support to the family and friends and the community, and to join those who are praying in the community," Masters said.

The e-mails, letters and public outpouring of sympathy for the boys, however, has had little impact on Golden's position about trying the boys as adults.

"Anyone who is guilty of first-degree murder, whether a juvenile or an adult, should never be in society again," Golden said. "They should be confined for the protection of the public. Juveniles physically and emotionally capable of committing a crime this serious should be restricted from ever being in society again. . . . It used to be unheard of that a twelve- or thirteen-year-old would have the ability to kill someone. It's changed."

Golden downplayed the intensity of the public complaints.

"It really hasn't been a deluge of requests," he said. "It hasn't been that heavy."

On the evening before Chavis's trial, Escambia County and much of Pensacola prepared for a media circus that was poised to converge on the community. Court TV would be there, and in fact had already begun setting up in the courtroom of Escambia County Circuit Judge Frank Bell, who would preside over both Chavis's trial as well as Alex and Derek's.

"Juveniles being tried as adults always spike an interest in our viewers," said Tom Donohue, Court TV's assignment manager. Donohue seemed particularly interested in the King brothers' trial because the boys appeared so young and innocent. "It's just amazing that they could, if they're guilty, have done such a heinous thing."

The network had spent much of the week of August 19 getting things ready in Judge Bell's courtroom.

"They do a great job," said Court Administrator

Wayne Peacock. "I just turn everything over to them. They're very professional."

Bell, meanwhile, said that he wasn't particularly concerned that the extensive coverage would create a "media circus."

"I've had a couple of trials that have been covered gavel-to-gavel, so to speak, and it didn't create any problems for me," Bell said. "And I don't think it had any effect on the way the case was tried, nor the results."

Bell modified his previous gag order and allowed the attorneys on both sides to speak with reporters with one condition: The reporters were required to sign an agreement that they would not reveal any of the attorneys' remarks until the trials had concluded.

Dateline NBC was planning on being there, as was CBS News, and CBS's *48 Hours*, among other shows.

If it had only been sweeps week.

CHAPTER 19

On Monday, August 26, 2002, the trial of Rick Chavis got under way in Courtroom 407 of the M. C. Blanchard Building, where the Escambia County courtrooms are located. Many people had made plans to attend the trials that would become known throughout the country as a three-ring circus, and some had even arranged to take time off from work to be there. This case was one that was not to be missed, particularly by those who had been following it from the outset.

Media trucks with satellite dishes positioned on top, along with tall antennas, surrounded the building. Traffic around the judicial building was reduced to a crawl, and security outside was being performed by deputies riding around on golf carts. With the sheriff's department on high alert, a mobile command unit—basically an oversized RV that had been outfitted with a video camera capable of revolving 360 degrees, television monitors, communications equipment like radios, telephones and fax machines, not to mention arms and munitions—was stationed outside as a precaution even though there had been no threats of violence or other problems. It was primarily for show, to act as a deterrent against any unforeseen problems that might arise.

The lawyers for both sides had arrived at the courthouse promptly at 9 A.M. They would work through the day and into the evening sifting through a pool of 139 potential jurors with their aim to seat two juries, one for Chavis's trial and one for Alex and Derek's. Chavis's trial would be held first, and the King boys' would follow. It had been decided early on that whatever verdict was reached in Chavis's trial would be sealed until after a verdict regarding Alex and Derek had been reached. The lawyers and the judge would be allowed to know the verdict of Chavis's trial, but no one else.

Wearing a gray suit and necktie, Chavis entered the courtroom and took his seat at the defense table. Exuding a certain charm, he smiled frequently at the jury pool, and appeared calm and relaxed.

Alex and Derek would also be in the courtroom while their jury was being selected, but only after Chavis's jury was seated and he had been removed. They, too, were dressed nicely in long-sleeved shirts, neckties and dress shoes, and when it was their turn, they, too, smiled at the jury pool. Derek also smiled for the cameras, and spoke occasionally to the deputies in the courtroom and to their attorneys, while Alex remained mostly quiet, apparently drawing or writing on a legal pad.

Earlier, during a hearing to determine whether to allow sexual abuse testimony, Judge Frank Bell had decided that testimony about the alleged sexual "relationship" between Chavis and Alex would be allowed during Chavis's trial, over the protestations of Chavis's attorney, Michael Rollo. Ruling that such testimony was "highly relevant" to the case, Bell had clearly made up his mind to allow it. "I think it does have some relevance to a jury," Bell ruled, "if Mr. Chavis and a witness had some kind of relationship, regardless of whether it was sexual or not."

Among the issues that the potential jurors would be questioned about was whether they could try children as young as Alex and Derek King as adults, whether they or anyone close to them had ever been a sexual abuse victim, their opinion as to whether a child can be influenced or manipulated by an adult and whether they could convict the children knowing that the boys could receive life sentences without possibility of parole.

The burning question that the juries would have to answer was: Who killed Terry King by beating him to death with a baseball bat and then attempted to cover up the crime by setting his house ablaze? For a jury, whether Chavis's or Derek and Alex's, to answer that question, it would have to decide who was the most believable, Rick Chavis or Alex and Derek King since each jury would be hearing nearly identical evidence and testimony.

There were no witnesses to the crime other than the killer(s), and any damning evidence that might have been available to investigators had disintegrated in the fire. Chavis's credibility was marred by his prior criminal record as a child molester, not to mention the fact that he had repeatedly changed the story he'd told to the cops. Similarly, Alex and Derek had changed their stories. There was also the possibility that their confessions to the police had been rehearsed. Chavis had eventually told the police that Alex and Derek had killed their father. Alex and Derek had told the grand jury that Chavis had killed him.

There was also the issue of the accelerants that had been poured around King's bedroom and then ignited. It would be brought out that a type of accelerant had been found on the boys' shoes, but it wasn't conclusively shown that it was the same accelerant that had been used to set the house ablaze. If the boys had not been present when their father had been killed, but had been waiting outside in the trunk of Chavis's car as they'd said, then how did they get accelerant on their shoes? As the juries would ponder this and other questions, who would they ultimately believe? .

Jury selection was an arduous process that continued throughout the day. Some jurors were excused when they indicated that they could not reach a verdict fairly because they were sympathetic with the children. One woman burst into tears as she heard details of the case, and other jurors were excused because they were not comfortable with hearing about the alleged sexual abuse against Alex.

By Monday evening, at approximately 8 P.M., two juries had been seated. The twelve-person jury that would hear Chavis's case consisted of seven women and five men, along with two alternates. A six-person jury for the boys consisted of three women and three men, along with four alternates.

The next day, Tuesday, August 27, Rick Chavis's trial began at 9 A.M. During his opening statement, Chavis's attorney, Michael Rollo, described Derek King as a "baby-faced" troublemaker and an incessant liar who had never developed a conscience. Rollo told the jury that a psychologist would be called to testify that, while Derek exhibited superficial charm, he frequently lied, showed little remorse or empathy for anyone he had victimized, and accepted no emotional responsibility for his actions— all signs, said Rollo, of a classic psychopath. Rollo also told the jury how Derek had lived with Frank and Nancy Lay for six years and how he proved to be a near-constant source of trouble for them. He said that Lay had wanted to send Derek to military school to correct his behavioral problems, but that Terry King had disagreed with that idea and said that he wanted to take Derek back home instead.

Emphasizing Derek's tendency to lie, Rollo told the jurors how the boys had changed their stories to the police after admitting that Alex had come up with the plan to kill their father and that Derek had carried it out. Rollo said they had changed their story for the grand jury that had indicted Chavis, and that their "new and improved" version was what they had come up with because they finally realized, after spending several months in jail, that they might be found guilty of killing their father.

"The way to solve it is the way that Derek likes to do things—to lie," Rollo told the jury.

Rollo contended that Terry King's death was the result of a "childlike, simplistic plan," and he urged the jury not to be taken in because of the innocent appearance of the two boys.

"They are guilty of the homicide," Rollo said. "Not Rick Chavis."

When it was Assistant State Attorney David Rimmer's turn to present his opening statement, he said that the sexual relationship between Alex and Chavis had been the defendant's motive for killing Terry King. Rimmer read to the jury some of what Alex had written to Chavis, professing his love for the convicted child molester. Rimmer emphasized part of one of Alex's notes, in which Alex had written: "Before I met Rick, I was straight. But now I am gay." Rimmer said that King had stopped his boys from visiting Chavis. Because of the strong relationship between the defendant and the boys, and the fact that he wanted the boys to live with him, he had killed King, Rimmer said.

Rimmer drew a diagram, using paper and an easel set up in the courtroom, that depicted his theory of Chavis as the murder suspect.

"They didn't want to be with their father," Rimmer told the jury. "They wanted to be with Ricky Chavis."

Following opening statements, the trial moved swiftly into testimony from witnesses.

Alex and Derek testified separately at Chavis's trial, and only one boy was allowed in the courtroom at a time. Alex, who had turned 13 in jail, took the witness stand. His hands remained cuffed as he struggled to reach the microphone by leaning into it. He spoke softly, his voice often barely audible, as he repeated how it had been Chavis, not he or Derek, who had swung the baseball bat that killed their father. He said Chavis did it so the boys could move in with him.

Alex said Chavis had told the boys that he would arrive at their house at midnight to pick them up. He and Derek had been told to leave the back door open so that Chavis could gain entry to the house without alerting their father, Alex testified. He would then surreptitiously take the boys out to his car, go back inside the house and kill King, and then take the boys home with him. That had been the plan, but it had been carried out somewhat differently, Alex explained.

Alex said that he and his brother had been playing board games while waiting for Chavis to arrive, but Derek had fallen asleep. A little later Chavis sneaked into the house and woke up Derek, instructing both boys to remain quiet. Alex told the court that Chavis had told him and Derek to sneak out through the back door and get inside the trunk of his Nissan Maxima and wait for him. Before they knew it, he said, they had arrived at Chavis's house and were let out of the trunk, at which time Chavis told them what had occurred, Alex said. Derek would later provide similar testimony.

"Why did you think you were gay?" Rimmer asked Alex at one point after again reminding the boy of what he had written about being homosexual.

"Because Ricky told me that," Alex responded. ". . . I was in love with Rick. I loved my dad."

Alex testified, as Derek would later, that Chavis had convinced the brothers that they had to take the fall for him because of their ages.

"He wanted us to take the blame because we could get off with self-defense," Alex testified. "He said, because he knew police officers could back us up on it. Told us the story, kept going over it."

Chavis remained passive as Alex testified. Nearly every eye in the gallery was upon the defendant while Alex, and later, Derek, testified about the alleged sexual relationship. He smiled when the issue of him smoking marijuana with the boys after their father's death was brought up.

Later, when Derek was sworn in, it was obvious from the faces of the spectators that they'd had a difficult time with the details brought out during Alex's testimony. Most people would later say that spectator reaction, which included many tears, was mostly due to the boys' ages, their baby faces and angelic appearance. Derek, who had turned 14 in jail, was also handcuffed. He seemed relaxed, however, stretching and sighing as he looked around the courtroom. As he leaned forward on his elbows to testify, he said that he could not recall all of the details surrounding the murder. He also said that he could not recall all of the details of his and Alex's confessions, or their grand jury testimony, and that he did not completely follow the line of questioning from the attorneys.

"It's been almost a year now since all of this has happened," Derek said, "and I really don't think about it."

Both Alex and Derek frequently responded to the attorneys' questions with answers like "I don't know," or "Can you repeat the question?" and "I can't remember." If these weren't children testifying in the new millennium, one might have associated them, or at least their testimony, with former U.S. Attorney General John Mitchell, or any of a host of other Watergate defendants during the Nixon era. One had to consider, of course, whether their attorneys had instructed them to respond in such a manner.

At one point Rimmer asked Derek about the weapon that Chavis was alleged to have used to kill King.

"He said that a bat had been involved," Derek responded.

Now it was Rollo's turn for cross-examination.

In response to questioning, Derek admitted that he remembered telling the investigators that he had struck his father in the head with a baseball bat ten times. When answering questions about his and Alex's life at home and what their father had been doing to make things better, tears were visible in Derek's eyes. He said that his father had planned on purchasing a television for them to place in one of their rooms.

"He said he'd make it better, and he would help us and make it better," Derek testified, "but he didn't have a chance to."

Both Alex and Derek testified that the only reason they had initially told the investigators that they had killed their father was so they could protect their friend, Rick Chavis.

Why had they changed their story?

"Because I didn't want to spend the rest of my life in prison covering for somebody else's acts," Derek testified. Derek said that he would be willing to do the prison time if he were truly guilty, and if his father's death "was the consequences of my actions."

At another point in Chavis's trial, arson investigator Kevin Fiedor, a lieutenant with the state fire marshal's office, explained that the fire set at King's home had been a "very simple" one. Under cross-examination from Rollo, Fiedor allowed that there might have been an underlying psychological reason that the fire had been set in Terry's bedroom. It was also suggested that Chavis, being an adult, would have set a fire that would have been much more devastating and destructive.

Fiedor also testified that his investigators tested the shoes that Alex and Derek had worn on the night of their father's slaying, and discovered the presence of paint thinner or some similar flammable liquid, but the accelerant found on their shoes could not be conclusively matched to the type found inside the house—they were only similar.

Alex and Derek had originally told Sanderson and Kilgore that they had left the aluminum baseball bat on the bed and had set the mattress beneath it ablaze. Fiedor testified that a fire in a room like King's bedroom could get as hot as 1800 to 2000 degrees, and he said that aluminum burns when it reaches 1200 degrees. Because only pieces of aluminum were discovered in King's bedroom, it was not possible to say conclusively that they were part of the baseball bat, which was believed destroyed in the fire.

Janice Johnson, a forensic specialist employed by the Escambia County Sheriff's Office, who helped investigate the crime scene, told the court that there were no signs of a struggle. She described how Terry King had been found, lying in his recliner with his feet propped up on a sofa, his hands folded and a coffee cup lying beside his lap. She said the evidence indicated that he had died right where he had been attacked. She said that there was blood on his body, blood spatter on the ceiling and on the floor next to him, as well as on the wall behind him and on a nearby lamp.

It was pointed out that Derek had previously confessed that he had crept up behind his sleeping father

and struck him repeatedly over the head with a baseball bat until brain matter could be seen. The expert
testimony appeared to point toward that scenario and
made the recanted confession a credible explanation
of how Terry King had been killed.

It was also pointed out that the boys had a *Lion
King* pillow and a *101 Dalmatians* blanket inside
their home at the time of their father's slaying.

At another point Rollo played Alex's and Derek's
taped confessions in their entirety. Rollo contended
that the details in their stories matched the details of
the crime scene, and as such, the boys must have
been inside the house and not in the trunk of Chavis's
car as they had testified. Earlier, while cross-
examining Detective Sanderson, Rollo suggested that
the vivid detail of the boys' confessions was proof
that they had been there, inside the house. Derek, he
noted, had told Sanderson and Kilgore that he had
found his dad sitting in a recliner, his feet "propped
up on the couch" and a cup of coffee in his hand.
Sanderson agreed with the defense attorney that that
was the precise position in which the investigators
had discovered King's body. Sanderson pointed out
that the boys had given a false version of their father's death prior to their later account, which was
consistent with what the investigators had found at
the crime scene.

In their first version, the boys told Sanderson that
their father was in the process of throwing Alex
around in the living room when Derek came running
in wielding a baseball bat. Derek said that he struck
his father with the bat and had knocked him off of
his feet and into the recliner, where he was found by
the firefighters and investigating deputies. That story

greatly conflicted with the crime scene: There was no sign of a struggle and investigators determined that King had died where he had been sitting while asleep. Furthermore, the only bloodstains found were near the recliner. Realizing that their story was false, Sanderson spoke to each of the boys separately and told them that he did not believe them.

"A crime scene tells a story," Sanderson said that he told Alex and Derek. "You need to tell us the truth."

A short time later, Sanderson testified, the brothers changed their story and provided the statement that was played in court. In that statement Alex had described how his father had "squeezed" his eyes shut in pain after the first blows.

"You could tell that he was in pain," Alex had said.

Alex described how his father began bleeding and how he struggled to breathe. He said that his father's face reflected his difficulty breathing as he exhaled, and that he made a sound similar to that of someone whose nose is plugged or congested.

Medical Examiner Gary Cumberland testified that Terry's last, pathetic gasps for air, as Alex described them, are what he and his associates call a "death rattle," and that it would not be likely for a person to be able to describe such an incidence as accurately as Alex had if that person had not been around someone who was dying.

"It's a pretty distinctive sound," Cumberland testified.

Having been fired earlier in the year by Sheriff Ron McNesby because of his friendship with Rick Chavis,

Deputy Reggie Jernigan had appealed his termination. After much negotiating, it was agreed in August that Jernigan would be rehired if he would drop the appeal, and he was assigned to courtroom security.

CHAPTER 20

The next day, Wednesday, August 28, Mike Chavis, Rick's brother, took the witness stand to testify about events in the hours immediately after Terry King's death. Responding to Rimmer's questions, he said that he had lived with his brother for years. On the night in question, they were both at home, sitting in their living room, when the phone rang shortly after 1:30 A.M. He explained that Rick had answered the phone with a surprised look and stood up as he asked, "What's wrong?" Moments later they heard about the fire on Muscogee Road over the police scanner in the living room. Rick, he said, had left hurriedly without saying anything, and returned some thirty minutes later with Alex and Derek. The boys, he testified, were carrying their clothes in their arms as they entered the mobile home.

"It was like Alex was in shock," Mike testified. "Couldn't talk. Derek seemed normal."

Derek then asked Rick if he wanted him to tell Mike what they had done, Mike testified. Derek explained how he had beaten his father with a baseball bat and afterward had set the house on fire. After Derek finished explaining what had occurred, the brothers placed their clothes in the washing machine and each took a shower. Afterward, they all went to sleep. Mike testified that he'd had a difficult time sleeping that night.

"I didn't know what state of mind Derek was in," he said. "I didn't know if he was going to do it to us, too. Any little noise and I opened my eyes."

Next, two juveniles who had been incarcerated with Alex and Derek testified that the boys told them about killing their father. One boy, 16, said that Alex and Derek had laughed when asked what they were in juvenile detention for. They said that they had been arrested for stealing, the boy testified. However, they later told the boy how Derek had repeatedly struck his father in the head with a baseball bat.

"It made me mad about it, them laughing about killing their dad," the boy said.

The other boy, also 16, told the court much what the first boy had, that both Alex and Derek had confessed to killing their father. He said that they had explained the killing in detail, describing how Derek had destroyed his dad's face and how blood sprayed everywhere.

"Then he said he just kept on hitting," the boy said.

Later, Rollo called Pensacola psychologist James Larson to the stand to explain the primary traits that a psychopath might display. Although Larson had never examined either of the boys, it became clear that Rollo was attempting to show that Derek displayed psychopathic tendencies. Larson explained that a psychopath frequently exhibits an ability to manipulate others, often displays restlessness, impulsiveness, charm and a lack of remorse. He said a psychopath also frequently has a high IQ but does poorly in school. It was pointed out that Derek's IQ had been established through tests to be in the 120 range. Although Larson could not definitively apply any of these characteristics to Derek, not having examined him, it was clear that Rollo would attempt to accomplish that task by following up Larson's testimony with that of Frank and Nancy Lay.

Frank Lay said he knew that Derek had problems and that when the boy had come to his house to live, he was carrying psychological "baggage" with him.

"They were not taken care of, that was obvious," Frank Lay said. "Those formative years are critical in the development of a child, and he didn't get it."

Although Lay and his wife had welcomed Derek into their 2,500-square-foot home with a swimming pool in the back yard, and had provided the boy with his own bedroom, a PlayStation, toys and permission to watch television, Derek had been a problem from the beginning. Lay said that the most important rule in their home was not to tell lies, and that was a rule that Derek broke repeatedly.

"The truth issue was constant," Lay said. "He has problems with that, big-time."

It wasn't just lying, however, according to Lay. Derek had been caught stealing a wallet at school, as well as other items, and had become a nuisance to his teachers. He had also grown increasingly fascinated by fire, and the Lays had frequently caught him in possession of cigarette lighters and matches. They also found firecrackers beneath his bed, and they became particularly alarmed on another occasion when they caught Derek filling a tiki torch with gasoline instead of the usual, less volatile kerosene.

"I didn't feel safe around him," Lay said.

At one point Rollo asked Lay a series of questions that were specific to the characteristics of a psychopath. He asked if Derek had shown any remorse for any of the things that he had been caught doing, knowing that they were against the rules.

"Very little," Lay responded.

"Was he able to manipulate others?" Rollo asked.

"He knew how to play that game," Lay said.

"Was he impulsive?" Rollo asked.

"Absolutely," Lay said.

"How well did Derek do in school?" Rollo asked.

"Poorly," Lay responded. "Then it got worse."

When Lay had suggested sending Derek to military school, Terry King had refused to allow it and said he wanted to take his son back home.

"You're not ready for this," Lay said he'd told King when he showed up to take Derek home with him.

Lay said that he was concerned about the sudden move back to Cantonment, leaving behind a middleclass home and environment for King's small house in a rural area.

"He was going from the penthouse to the outhouse," Lay said.

Rollo questioned Lay about the first time Derek and Alex had run away from King's home, and the encounter that Lay had with Derek after his whereabouts were discovered on November 25, 2001. He said that Derek had pleaded with him not to send him back to his father's house because his father was a "control freak."

"I can't go back to my dad's house," Lay quoted Derek as saying. "I can't go back. . . . Alex hates my dad. He hates him. He said he'd like to see him dead."

Nancy Lay also testified, describing Derek, when he was 6 years old, as a "Dennis the Menace." She said that he had broken nearly every rule that she and her husband had tried to apply. Nancy also corroborated her husband's testimony about Alex wanting his father dead.

"You can't send us back, because my brother's going to kill him," Nancy Lay quoted Derek as saying. "We already have a plan."

That same day Alex and Derek's mother, going by the legal name of Kelly Marino, but also known as Janet French, was in court to testify at Chavis's trial. It was an awkward situation for her because she would be testifying against her own sons. After being sworn in, she briefly testified that Derek had informed her that he and Alex had killed their father. Derek had made the admission to her when she had visited the boys in the juvenile detention center a few days after Terry's death.

Later, Marino told reporters for the *Pensacola News Journal* that she really believed that Chavis had killed Terry King. She said that she reached that conclusion because she had asked Derek why he had killed his dad, but he could not provide an answer. Instead, he had only shrugged his shoulders. She said that she had no choice, however, other than to truthfully testify as to what Derek had told her at the juvenile detention center. She said that she would never do anything to hurt her children.

"I never stopped taking care of my children and

loving them," Marino tearfully told the reporter. "I'm very nurturing. Very hugging. Very loving. . . . Me and Terry, we were children having children."

She said that she and Terry, whom she described as her "first love," had done the best under their circumstances. She said that she had not been able to marry King during the eight years that they were together because he was married to someone else.

Marino, who said she was working toward a private investigator's license, also said that she did not believe the taped statement that Alex and Derek had made to the investigators. Instead, she said she thought the boys had been manipulated by Chavis, and that they were drawn to him because they could watch television and play video games at his home.

"I think the boys wanted all that fun over there at Rick's," she told the reporter. "I don't think they had anything to do with the murder. But, of course, I'm their mom."

Marino claimed that one of the reasons she had had a difficult time with Alex and Derek was that she had suffered from postpartum depression. She claimed that she was still depressed, and that her depression was now intensified because of everything that had happened, and because of the trials.

Marino said that she disagreed with the Lays' contention that Derek had had problems, lied constantly and was manipulative.

"I just wanted to jump up there and say, 'It's not true! It's not true,' " she said. She said that when she called the Lay residence and attempted to talk to Derek, she was often told that he was either at school or was out playing with his friends.

"I called constantly to check in the beginning,"

Marino said. "We upset his routine, we were told, and it took him several days to calm down."

Marino said that she strongly disagreed with defense attorney Michael Rollo characterizing Derek as a psychopath. She described Derek as a gentle teenager who happened to suffer from attention deficit hyperactivity disorder and who needed Ritalin, which was not being provided to him in jail.

"My son is not a psychopath," she stated. "That is insane."

CHAPTER 21

Later, after the prosecution rested its case, Judge Bell heard a motion of dismissal by defense attorney Michael Rollo. As do all defense attorneys, Rollo presented the motion to throw out the murder charges against Chavis because of the chilling statement Alex and Derek had made to police in which they had confessed to killing their father. The details were so intimate, they left little doubt that the boys had been inside the house when their father was killed. Based on the intricate details that the brothers had provided in their statement, which had been played in court, Rollo just didn't believe that Chavis was guilty of murder.

While Judge Bell agreed that there wasn't much evidence tying Chavis to King's death, and even less that pointed toward him trying to coax Alex and Derek into killing their father, he said that there was sufficient evidence that pointed toward Chavis being involved after the killing. That was the reason Chavis had been charged with being an accessory after the fact to murder following the first grand jury proceedings on December 11, 2001.

By now it was evident to all concerned that the prosecution's case against Rick Chavis was flimsy at best, particularly the murder charges. It seemed like Chavis had been charged with murder in an attempt to get him to talk. If that had been the prosecution's plan, it had backfired embarrassingly.

"There's plenty of evidence in this trial of what he did after the fact," Bell said. "But he's charged with that, and that trial is to be decided at a later time."

Bell denied Rollo's motion to dismiss all the murder charges. The judge did, however, place limitations on the tactics Prosecutor Rimmer could use in obtaining a guilty verdict. When the trial began, the jury could have convicted Chavis under two theories of law. One could have shown Chavis as the perpetrator who actually killed King with a baseball bat and set his house ablaze afterward; the other could have shown him a principal in the case, in which he had encouraged Alex and Derek to commit the slaying and/or had assisted the boys in carrying out the crime. Bell, in his ruling, threw out the principal theory by saying that there was "zero in this record that he did that" to support it, that "it's just not there."

In almost every criminal trial the defense attorney asks the judge to dismiss the charges. It usually never happens. It was remarkable that Bell actually threw out some of the charges against Chavis, giving the defense at least a partial victory.

Rimmer earlier had admitted that the case against Chavis was "not my strongest."

After sending the jury out of the courtroom, Bell

and the attorneys discussed a very unusual aspect of the case: It was possible that the separate juries could find Chavis, as well as Alex and Derek, guilty of Terry King's slaying.

"Is it possible for two different juries to find both of them guilty?" Bell asked. "Yes. Is it possible for two different juries to find both of them not guilty? Yes. Is it possible for two different juries to find one of them guilty and the other one not guilty? Yes. Unusual. Very unusual."

Later, after the jury was brought back into the courtroom, Rollo's defense of Chavis centered around Alex's and Derek's confessions that they, not Chavis, had carried out a plan to kill their father. There was no physical evidence that pointed toward Chavis as the killer.

In his closing argument, Rollo said Alex's and Derek's testimony against Chavis was merely an effort to save their own skins after they realized that their original account of what happened would likely land them in prison. Rollo emphasized that Sanderson and Kilgore had previously stated earlier in the investigation, after they had begun to focus on Chavis as a possible suspect, that they would have arrested Chavis earlier if they had had any evidence to back them up. Rollo drove home the point that Chavis was not arrested until after the boys had changed their story and had testified before a grand jury in April.

"Who are you going to trust?" Rollo asked. "Trust the officers. They got it right. We don't like to say that children with cherubim faces can be cold, calculating, homicidal psychopaths."

Rollo, urging that the jury find Chavis innocent of murder and arson in Terry King's death, told the jury that there was "no evidence . . . zero. None," that his client had committed the crimes for which he'd been charged, and that there was no evidence that Chavis had been at King's house when King was killed. He drove home the point that the judge had disallowed the theory that would have let Chavis be convicted as a principal in the case.

"What you're going to have to do here," Rollo said, "is take the principal theory and put it where it belongs."

Rollo then tore off a page from an easel that was set up in the courtroom in which the prosecutor had previously drawn a diagram that depicted the theory of showing Chavis as a principal in the case. Rollo wadded it up into a ball and threw it into a wastebasket.

"It doesn't matter now that the co-defendants . . . may have committed the murder themselves," Rollo said. "You have to determine whether he [Chavis] did it. Whether he actually wielded the bat."

Prosecutor Rimmer's closing argument was brief— and unusual. Rimmer did not tell the jury that Chavis had been the person who had swung the bat that killed King, and he did not tell the jury that they should believe what Alex and Derek had testified to in court. He never asked the jury to find Chavis guilty, either.

"We're here because the King boys lied," Rimmer said. "They either lied to the police, or they lied to you. I'm going to let you decide. I don't have a dog in this fight . . . my only concern is that justice be done."

Rimmer's closing argument took less than five minutes to complete.

The jury was not sequestered, and Judge Bell gave them permission to go home that Thursday evening, August 29, before returning to the courtroom the following morning to begin their deliberations. The judge gave the jury four options in deciding Chavis's fate. They could find him guilty of first-degree murder, second-degree murder, manslaughter or not guilty. Chavis, the judge had said, could only be convicted if the jury determined that he actually wielded the bat. The state had not provided sufficient evidence to prove that Chavis had prior knowledge of the crime.

The jury returned the following day and began deliberations. At one point, they sent a message to the judge asking for a legal definition for an "intentional act" as it pertained to manslaughter. Bell rejected the jury's request and ordered them to continue their deliberations. About five hours after they began, the jury returned to the courtroom and announced that they had reached a verdict. They handed a sealed envelope to the bailiff, who in turn gave it to the judge. Bell ordered that the verdict remain sealed and locked away until after verdicts against Alex and Derek were reached. Their trial was set to begin the following Tuesday morning in the same courtroom. Bell also told the jurors that they were prohibited from speaking about the case, their deliberations or their verdict until after the verdicts were reached in the King brothers' trial. "Please, just tell them [anyone who asks] that you're under an oath that you took as a juror not to disclose that information," Bell said.

Afterward, Rimmer told reporters that he had never tried a case involving a sealed verdict in his twenty years as a prosecutor. "At this stage," Rimmer said, "I don't know if I really want to know [the verdict]. It might mess up my mind over the weekend."

The prosecutor said that he was still working to shut out feelings of sympathy for the boys because of their ages, and that, although the evidence would be "adequate" for a jury to decide their innocence or guilt, the jurors would still have to struggle with similar problems: overcoming their sympathy for the boys, and facing potential public scorn if they returned a guilty verdict.

"People look at them," Rimmer said. "They look at them and form impressions."

The Escambia County Sheriff's Department indicated that they expected children's rights activists to be at Alex and Derek's trial along with relatives and curious locals. *People* magazine had also grabbed on to the story and had their reporters in town to cover the event that the entire nation was now talking about.

CHAPTER 22

As preparations were being made for Alex and Derek's trial, there was much talk about the evidence that would be presented. Speculation centered on Alex's expected testimony, the prosecutor's two opposing theories of Terry King's murder and how they applied to both Chavis's trial and that of the two brothers. Legal experts were saying that it was rare for a prosecutor to have separate trials to prosecute a case under two distinct theories of what had happened and who had committed the crime.

Much of the trial would consist of what had been heard and shown at the previous one, except that Chavis's defense would be turned around and presented as evidence against Alex and Derek. Because of everything that was brought out during Chavis's trial, most of the legal analysts showing up almost daily on MSNBC, CNN, and Court TV agreed that the evidence against Alex and Derek was strong. Similarly, those who had followed Chavis's trial expected prosecutor David Rimmer's demeanor at Alex and Derek's trial to be significantly different.

"It's still the same case," Rimmer responded after being asked by reporters how his strategy might differ in the King brothers' trial. "The facts are the facts. Things can always change in terms of trial strategy and the order in which you call witnesses. You can call or not call some witnesses, or call on different witnesses."

In addition to the confessions the boys made to Sanderson and Kilgore, it was all but certain that this trial would include testimony from Frank and Nancy Lay, both of whom had testified that Derek's behavior had frightened them. They were also certain to testify again that Alex had instigated—and Derek had agreed to—a plot to kill their father in part because of his perceived strictness. Alex had stated that he hated his father and wanted to see him dead.

As the nation listened and watched, wondering what the verdicts would be, everyone was abuzz in Pensacola with talk of the murder and the trials. No matter where one went, whether to a local café or a local barber shop, the case was all that people were talking about.

"It has everything you want—murder, mystery, homosexuality," said one Pensacola businessman.

Another local, struck by the boys' young ages and their angelic appearances, said she had her doubts about their guilt, particularly Alex's.

"You look at him, and he looks like an angel," said the resident. "They both look like choirboys."

She said that she was troubled at how Alex's confession had seemed to have been rehearsed and was absent any emotion. She said that his testimony at Chavis's trial had struck her the same way, and it had bothered her that he had shown no remorse and shed no tears over his father's death. The woman's husband, however, told a reporter that he did not believe the two were innocent. He said that Alex's and Derek's confessions were so vivid and full of detail, that the boys must have been at the scene of the crime.

Another Pensacola businessman cited the Kings' broken home, the fact that Derek had spent so much time in foster care and that neither of the boys had seen their mother in several years. He said that it was conceivable that the boys could commit murder.

"I don't know whether they did it or not," the businessman said. "But I know eleven- and twelve-year-olds are capable of it."

The trial got under way on Tuesday, September 3. In an unusual move in a case that had been nothing but unusual, Rick Chavis took the stand moments before David Rimmer was to give his opening statement. After the jury was ordered out of the courtroom, Chavis calmly declared his Fifth Amendment right against self-incrimination. Clearly, he would not be testifying at Alex and Derek's trial.

After the jury returned to the courtroom, Rimmer began his opening statement. Facing the jurors, Rimmer took them step-by-step through the case, beginning with the call to firefighters at 1:39 A.M. on November 26, 2001. He described the scene, how King's body was found, and how Alex and Derek had disappeared. He explained how Chavis had shown up at the sheriff's office the following day with both of the boys, claiming that they had been hiding out in the woods and had called him asking for a ride. He described how the boys had told the investigators that there had been a fight between their father and Alex, and that things had gotten out of hand when Terry King flung Alex to the floor. Later, he said, Derek had attacked his father with a baseball bat after he had gone to sleep, striking him numerous times until he was dead. He said that Alex had come up with the idea to kill their father.

Alex, sitting at the defense table, looked down as he wrote or drew pictures on a yellow legal pad that his lawyer had provided him.

"They said their father was playing mind games, mentally abusing them, staring them down, things of that nature," Rimmer told the jury. "The evidence is going to show that Alex . . . wanted his father dead and encouraged Derek to do it."

It took the silver-bearded prosecutor barely five minutes to finish his opening statement.

James Stokes, Alex's lawyer, told the jury in his opening statement that the taped confession that Alex and Derek had made to Sanderson and Kilgore was merely a result of Chavis's manipulation—telling them what to say to the police. Stokes then asked Alex to stand up so that the jurors could see the 13-year-old boy with the baby face while Stokes described the sexual relationship alleged to have begun two years earlier.

"He first told Alex," Stokes said as he walked back and forth in front of the jury box, "and then both boys, that their father was staring at them. Their father was yelling at them when they did something wrong. That that was mental abuse. Ricky Chavis, once he began his relationship with Alex, he started telling Alex that . . . 'Terry King can't love you the way I can. You are a very special child, Alex.' "

Stokes said Chavis was becoming apprehensive,

worrying that Terry King was suspicious about his relationship with Alex and Derek. Chavis, the defense attorney said, had come up with a plan to kill King and then set fire to his house to cover up the crime. According to Stokes, Chavis was afraid he'd have to go back to jail if King discovered the truth about his relationship with Alex.

"He knows if that relationship is discovered, he will go to prison forever," Stokes said, also reminding the jury of Chavis's 1984 conviction for child molestation.

The plan to kill King, Stokes told the jury, involved Chavis instructing Alex to unlock the back door of his house before going to bed on the night in question. Stokes said that Chavis entered the house during the early morning hours, after Terry and the boys had returned home from visiting Terry's friend, Lewis Tyson. He then sent Alex and Derek out to his car, killed Terry, and set the house on fire.

The plan, however, had become skewed when firefighters showed up in response to a neighbor's 911 call, and extinguished the fire before it could consume the room where Terry had been killed, and where his body lay, Stokes said. When that occurred, Stokes said, Chavis told Alex and Derek that they were just as guilty as he was and convinced them that they had less to lose than him because they were juveniles and could always claim self-defense or abuse. He persuaded them to make false confessions to the police in order to protect him.

Sharon Potter, Derek's lawyer, asked the jurors to maintain an open mind to the case as evidence was presented. She told them that the evidence would demonstrate that the prosecution's case against the boys was flawed.

During the morning hours of the trial's opening day, the prosecution presented seven witnesses in rapid succession, including Frank and Nancy Lay and juveniles from the detention center who testified about what the boys had told them.

"He [Derek] told me that he just got mad at his dad because he didn't want to get beat anymore," said one of the juveniles, "so he just killed his dad with a baseball bat. He told me his brother, Alex King, planned it."

Mike Chavis, Rick's brother, also testified. He repeated much of the same testimony that he'd given in his brother's trial by describing how his brother had gone out to pick up the boys to bring them home after they'd called him. He said that Derek had told him that he had attacked his dad.

"He said he hit his dad over the head with a bat," Mike Chavis testified.

Sharon Potter suggested that Mike Chavis was trying to protect his brother because he relied on Rick Chavis for financial support.

Stokes, at one point, brought up the alleged sexual relationship between Rick Chavis and Alex. Stokes contended that both Mike and Derek were present when Rick had held Alex on his lap and kissed him. Mike, however, was insistent that he had only seen hugging between Alex and Rick. Mike did say that his brother had shown interest in having a relationship with Alex, but that he'd planned to wait until Alex turned 16.

Theresa Schumate, a longtime friend of the boys' mother, Janet French, also testified that she had heard

Derek confess to killing his father. She said she heard
it when she accompanied the boys' mother on a visit
with Derek the day of Terry King's funeral. "He said
he killed his father with a ball bat and that he hit him
about ten times," Schumate testified. "During this, he
was crying. He was very, very upset."

At another point in the trial, the jury heard testimony about whether or not either of the boys had the
physical capability to beat their father's head in with
a bat. It was brought out at trial that Rick Chavis had
at one time, shortly before King's death, owned an
old, stripped-down car that he was planning to sell
for scrap metal. One afternoon, when Terry King
brought Alex and Derek over to Chavis's house, the
boys had asked Chavis if they could beat the car with
a sledgehammer they had found on the premises.
Chavis, and apparently the boys' father, had given
their consent, and the boys had taken turns using the
eight-pound sledge to further demolish the old car,
denting it all over and smashing its windows out.
Derek, it was revealed, had beaten the car with such
force that he had split the hammer's wooden handle.

The prosecution's case against Alex and Derek
clearly wasn't built on forensic evidence, but on
statements that the boys had made to the police and
to friends, relatives and other juvenile inmates. Rimmer nonetheless called forensic witnesses who testified that Terry King was most likely asleep in the
recliner where his body was found. One of those witnesses, Reginald Hutchins, a forensic analyst, testified about the shoes Alex and Derek wore on the
night their father was killed.

According to Hutchins, the shoes worn by both
boys contained traces of a flammable liquid that he

called an "aromatic solvent." However, forensics tests on debris from the fire turned up traces of a different type of accelerant. Although it was not specifically identified, Hutchins said that it had a petro-leum base.

Kevin Fiedor, a state fire marshal, had testified at Chavis's trial that the substance on the shoes chemically resembled paint thinner. Whoever had started the fire, he said, had poured some kind of an accelerant over much of King's bedroom before lighting it. However, no one said whether the accelerant that had ignited in King's bedroom had been paint thinner.

Both of the defense attorneys maintained that the supposed paint thinner was left over from a recent house-painting project. Alex had said that he and Derek had helped their father paint their house just before running away from home on November 16, 2001.

Janice Johnson, an Escambia County Sheriff's Department forensics expert, testified regarding evidence found near King's body. She described blood spatter on the floor, the walls, a lampshade nearby and on the body itself. Johnson said that the blood spatter suggested King had been killed in the recliner where his body was found. She also testified that the bloodstained lampshade next to King's body had a sizeable dent. That seemed to have been explained with Alex's claim that Derek missed his father when swinging the bat the second time.

At another point during the morning session, the jurors were shown crime-scene photos, some of which depicted Terry King as he was found. Alex and Derek did not seem particularly disturbed by that, or by anything else that was occurring during their trial. While the jury viewed the photos, Alex and Derek fidgeted in their chairs. It was either nervous action disguised, or neither boy had a clue what was occurring around them. During a brief morning recess, Alex and Derek talked with each other, often smiling, while their lawyers were out of the courtroom, but they quickly resumed their prior behavior when everyone filed back in.

CHAPTER 23

The next day, Wednesday, September 4, Escambia County Deputy Sheriff Thomas Mohan testified that when he returned Derek to his father the day before the killing, Derek had asked him what he needed to do to file an abuse claim against his father.

"He told me that he is never allowed to watch TV and that his father is very picky about his friends," Mohan testified. "I said that in my eyes, that's being a good parent."

At one point during the boys' trial, the six-member jury got to listen to Alex's and Derek's taped confessions to the police, just as the jury in Chavis's trial had. They heard Alex calmly explain to Detectives John Sanderson and Terry Kilgore that he wanted Derek to kill Terry, because of the mental and physical abuse that they believed their father was committing. As Alex listened and doodled on the yellow legal pad, jurors heard his recorded voice describe how "it was obvious that he was dead," and "a little bit of his brains was on the wall." The jurors also heard Alex claiming to have thought up the idea of killing his father.

"I feel mainly responsible," Alex said in the taped interview. "Derek took the hits . . . but I was the one that gave him the idea."

When James Stokes cross-examined Sanderson about the police interviews, he drove home his point that the boys' attitudes when they provided their statements seemed "carefree" and that they both described the alleged abuse by their father in nearly identical terms. The defense attorney was attempting to show that Alex and Derek's claims of abuse and self-defense rang hollow—and that they may have been calling for someone else.

"We don't have much abuse in the story, do we?" Stokes asked Sanderson.

"Not a lot," the detective responded.

Stokes continued to suggest that Alex had gone out of his way to protect Chavis, and that that was why he confessed to murder, setting the house afire and destroying evidence. He said that there appeared to be inconsistencies in the boys' statements, and said that the investigators should have done more to get at the truth than merely accepting their confessions at face value. Stokes also insinuated that the detectives should have had their suspicions about Chavis aroused earlier in the case, particularly since he was a convicted child molester who early on had told the police that he had washed the clothes that the boys wore when their father was killed.

Sanderson responded that the boys' descriptions of the crime scene had been much too accurate to have been made up.

"To me," Sanderson said, "we didn't have inconsistencies."

At another point Escambia County Medical Examiner Gary Cumberland testified about Terry King's cause of death. Cumberland said that King had suffered a fractured skull, a torn nostril, a torn scalp that left brain matter exposed beneath the fractured skull, and four individual bruises on his chest. The prosecutor asked him to read a transcript of Alex's description of the attack, then asked whether Alex's description had been consistent with Cumberland's findings.

"What he described," Cumberland responded, "would be consistent with being there at the time the injuries were inflicted."

During cross-examination, Dennis Corder, Sharon Potter's co-counsel, asked Cumberland whether Alex could have been provided all of the details about the crime scene based on something he heard from another person.

"He certainly could have been told those things by someone who had been there, isn't that right?" Corder asked.

"Yes, sir," Cumberland responded.

Later that day, Judge Bell sent the jury out of the courtroom for approximately thirty minutes while he and the attorneys conferred about a new witness, a 13-year-old boy in the eighth grade who had said that Derek had told several children on a school bus that he and his brother were going to kill their dad. Judge Bell questioned the boy about what he had heard on the bus that day.

"One day," the boy said, "Derek was getting in trouble because he was touching a girl. As he was

getting off the bus he told us that they (Alex and
Derek) were going to be gone for a while and that
we were going to hear about [them] on the news because they were going to kill their dad, and then they
were going to kill us." The 13-year-old boy's testimony was not presented to the jury.

As a witness in his own defense, Alex testified
later in the day after the jury returned to the courtroom. Sometimes speaking so softly that his voice
was barely audible, Alex told the jury that he had
lied to the police when he had confessed to them.
Alex also said that Chavis had told them that their
father did not care for them, and that Terry King was
not Alex's biological father. Chavis, Alex said, had
told him and his brother that he had discovered that
fact while doing "research" about the family. "We
were on the subject of my dad," Alex testified. "He
said he [Terry] didn't appreciate me and stuff. Rick
said he loved me. He said we were different and stuff.
We were gay."

Amid gasps and tears from the spectators, Alex
told the jury that Chavis had said it was "normal" for
men and boys to kiss. Alex said that he had slept in
Chavis's room during the nine days that he was hiding out from his father.

He said that Chavis had told him a lot of men and
boys had sex together and that it satisfied a natural
curiosity. Alex again said that he was "in love" with
Chavis, and explained how he and his brother had
stayed hidden at Chavis's home for several days after
they ran away. They had hidden beneath a trap door
in one of the bedrooms and remained there, out of
sight, when their father had come around looking for
them.

"I wanted to be with Rick because I was in love with Rick," Alex testified. He said that Chavis let him and his brother play video games whenever they liked, and allowed them to watch television as late as they wanted. He also provided marijuana and allowed them to smoke it—as well as cigarettes—at his home, Alex said. It was while he and his brother were staying at Chavis's home, Alex said, that he fell in love with the older man.

Alex told the jurors that his father had seemed happy to have the boys back home on the night he was killed, and that he made no threats to spank or discipline them, a stark contrast from what he had told the police. As he had done at the earlier trial, Alex testified that Chavis had told him to unlock the back door to their house. When Chavis entered early that morning, Alex said, he told the two boys to go outside and get into his car. They got into the car's trunk by letting down the back seat. A short time later, Alex said, Chavis got into the car and drove them to his home.

"He told us that there had been a fight between him and my dad, and he said that dad was dead," Alex testified. "He was saying it was terrible. . . . He said that it'll be all right because the fire would burn everything up. . . .

"He was saying he had done it for us . . . he said he had killed my dad to protect us. . . . He said my dad would never have let us live with him, that he'd never let us go. . . . I was crying, and I was upset. Kind of angry at him [Chavis] . . . for saying that he had done it for me. . . . He said that if we took the blame, we would get off on self-defense because we were juveniles."

"We have heard a very different story that you gave the police," Stokes said. "Where did you get this detailed story from?"

"Rick," Alex stated. "We were going over it constantly. I would go over it, and he would correct us. And then Derek would go over it, and he would correct us."

Alex said they stayed up late smoking marijuana and going over the story the boys would tell police.

"He went over all the details," Alex said. "He said how to describe it all. Kept going over it until we got it all right."

Stokes asked whether the boys had agreed to take the blame right away.

"No, sir," Alex responded. "It was some time before we agreed to take the story, to take the blame."

Alex told the jury that everything had gone off according to plan at first. He said that he and his brother had even called Chavis from the juvenile detention center to make certain that the plan was still in motion. It wasn't until Alex and Derek had been charged as adults, on December 11, and had been transferred to the adult jail that they began having doubts about Chavis's plan, Alex said.

"Alex, did you love your father?" Stokes asked.

"Yes, sir," Alex responded.

"Were you in the room when he was killed that night?" Stokes asked.

"No, sir," Alex said.

"Did Derek kill your father?" Stokes asked.

"No, sir."

Next up was Tony Bain, an Escambia County Sheriff's Department sergeant and former criminal investigator for the navy, who was in charge of the crime scene. He said Chavis had returned to King's home around 3:30 A.M. the morning King died, and had asked a sheriff's deputy what had happened and if the person in the house was dead.

"He asked me if it was Terry," Bain said. "He asked me if we thought that Terry had committed suicide."

Bain told Chavis that it was much too early in the investigation to make that kind of determination, he testified.

" 'Do you think maybe those boys did it?' " Bain said Chavis had asked him.

Glenn Gowitzke, an Escambia County Sheriff's Department investigator, was the next person to take the witness stand. He told the court that he had not found any evidence of a baseball bat in the burned-out house. Alex and Derek stated in their confessions that they had placed the aluminum baseball bat on the bed before setting the mattress on fire. Gowitzke said that a piece of melted aluminum had been found in the room, but it was of cheap quality, similar to the aluminum used in window frames, not the kind that would be used in a baseball bat. Aluminum used in baseball bats needs to be of high quality, strong, so that it can hold up when hitting baseballs.

Gowitzke said that he had discovered child pornography on Chavis's computer when he had inspected it.

Derek did not testify.

It was time for closing arguments. Prosecutor David Rimmer asked the jury to find Alex and Derek King guilty of premeditated murder. Although Rimmer characterized Chavis as the "motivator" of the crime, he described Alex as the mastermind and Derek as the killer who'd swung the bat.

"Derek is the one who actually carried it out," Rimmer said. "He is the one who inflicted the fatal blows."

Rimmer urged the jury not to be influenced by Alex's and Derek's ages.

"When you begin your deliberations," Rimmer said, "you can't go back there and say, 'Those poor boys. They're so young. How could they do this horrible thing? I just can't convict them.' It would be a miscarriage of justice."

Rimmer urged the jurors to think about Alex's ability to "recall the deadly details." He also read a letter that Alex had written to his father, which had been found by investigators after the boys' arrests. In it he had described his home as a prison. The letter had apparently been written as a means to vent his frustrations to his father about the strict living conditions at the King home.

"He doesn't want to live in that prison," Rimmer said about Alex's motivation. "He wants to be with Rick. His father told him he would never see Rick again."

Rimmer also cautioned the jurors against basing their decision on their feelings about Chavis. He said that their verdict should not be based on anger towards Chavis.

"Nobody likes Chavis," Rimmer said. "Chavis is the kind of guy everybody wants to hate. What's lower than a child molester? Judge them by their actions, not their ages. Judge them by their intent, not emotions." Rimmer rested.

Now it was Stokes's turn.

"If Rick Chavis did not convince the boys to take the blame for this, who would have been the primary suspect?" Stokes asked. "Rick Chavis needed the boys to make that confession, or the police would have been on him, and he knew that."

Derek's lawyer, Sharon Potter, got the last word with the jury.

"Ricky Chavis was obsessed with Alex King, this child sitting over here at this table," she said. "Derek had no motive to kill his father," she said, reiterating how he had only been reunited with his father for a short time when King was killed. Like Stokes, Potter pointed the finger at Chavis.

"They loved it at his house," Potter said. "TV, video games, no chores, no school, no church, marijuana, McDonald's. A kid's dream come true."

After Potter finished, Judge Bell charged the jury with its obligations, and they left the courtroom to begin their deliberations. They could find the boys guilty of first-degree murder, second-degree murder, first-degree murder without a weapon, second-degree murder without a weapon, manslaughter, or not guilty. The references to "without a weapon" meant that the jury could find them guilty merely because of their involvement in being present during the commission of a murder without actually committing the murder themselves.

CHAPTER 24

As the jurors decided Alex's and Derek's fate, the intensity of speculation about the case—among the public and in legal circles—reached a fever pitch. Dennis Corder, Derek's co-counsel, all but accused Rimmer of prosecutorial misconduct for trying to convict three people for a single murder.

"They prosecuted one, and now they're prosecuting another," Corder said. "Prosecutors cannot just prosecute until they get a conviction. . . . We think that violates due process. . . . Prosecutors have a duty beyond that of regular lawyers to seek the truth."

"The only reason Mr. Chavis ever got indicted was because of what the King boys did," Rimmer countered, referring to Alex and Derek changing their original story and testifying against Chavis before a grand jury.

What would happen if both Chavis and the King brothers were all convicted of killing King? Many people had asked the question, and the way the case was handled had created something of a legal dilemma.

"It's not unusual to have co-defendants to a murder," wrote CBSNews.com's legal analyst Andrew Cohen. "What's unusual is to have separate trials in which the government's theories of the case contradict each other. Either the boys did it or Chavis did but all three could not have done it if you buy the prosecution's argument and that means big problems for the State on appeal if there are convictions in both cases."

Mark Seidenfeld, associate dean at Florida State University law school, and Christopher Slobogin, a law professor at the University of Florida, both agreed that the prosecutor should have decided who he wanted to prosecute and taken only one case to trial.

"It's on the verge of being unethical that they would pursue contradictory theories when they are relatively sure that the evidence points to one . . ." Slobogin said. He added that it would not be unconstitutional to have contradictory verdicts, and that such verdicts could be upheld on appeal.

"Sometimes prosecutors forget what their role is," Seidenfeld said. "I sometimes think that they're trying only to get convictions. . . ."

While the 2nd jury was out, Judge Bell had fretted over the legal implications of the case. If both juries turned in guilty verdicts, three people would go to jail for the same crime when, at must, only two could have actually committed it. Bell had decided to call all of the attorneys together in private hearings to discuss the matter.

"We all know that either the King brothers are not guilty or Mr. Chavis is not guilty," Bell told the attorneys.

"I do not want to impose a sentence on somebody that we know is not guilty," Bell continued. "I'm just not going to do that. . . . I mean, whether it be Mr. Chavis or the King boys, that would be a horrible thing . . . I'm just not going to do that. . . . We're not talking about thirty days in the county jail for disorderly conduct here."

Bell's point, of course, was that the charges being discussed were far more serious than disorderly conduct and his as well as the lawyers' duties should not be taken lightly.

Bell also pondered whether a guilty verdict against Chavis would prevent the state from going ahead with its case against Alex and Derek. If Chavis could have been convicted as a principal at his trial, then there wouldn't be a problem, the judge told the attorneys. Since Bell had ruled out such a possibility when he decided that Chavis would not be prosecuted as a principal, but only as a perpetrator, there could be a problem, depending on the verdict that Chavis's jury might arrive at. What if Chavis's jury found Chavis guilty of first-degree murder and the King boys jury found them guilty of identical charges?

"Can the state go forward . . . and prosecute once we have a judicial determination by a jury that you asked to convict in a who-do-you-believe alternative?" Bell asked Rimmer.

Rimmer had been unable to respond because he had not known the answer.

Even though Bell had announced that the verdict in Chavis's case would remain sealed until after the King jury had reached its verdict, he changed his mind and called another meeting with the attorneys to discuss the consequences should the verdict, which he now held in his hands, be a guilty one. After admonishing the attorneys to promise not to reveal the verdict to anyone, including their clients, Bell decided to open the envelope.

"I can't think of any problems this might cause," he had said. "Can anyone?"

The judge then opened the envelope and read the not-guilty verdict. He sighed with relief.

"Well, that obviously takes care of my concerns," Bell had said.

There was also the question of what would happen to Alex and Derek, regardless of the outcome of their trial. If acquitted, where would they live? Janet French, also known as Kelly Marino, the boys' mother, told reporters that she would want the boys to live with her and her husband, since she had legal custody of them. Behind the state of Florida, that is.

"The plans are for them to be with me," Marino said. "After all this, it would be kind of nice not to be right in the area [of Pensacola]."

Even before King's death, Marino said that she and her husband had been planning to move to Florida so that she could be closer to her boys.

On the other hand, if Alex and Derek were convicted, they would be sent to the North Florida Reception Center in Lake Butler, according to Sterling Ivey, spokesman for the state's Department of Corrections. Upon their arrival, screeners would run psychological and medical evaluations to determine which of the state's five facilities for young offenders would be most fitting. There were two prisons that only take inmates under 18 years of age.

"For kids thirteen and fourteen years old," Ivey

said, "prison may not be the appropriate place for them to serve their time."

Regardless of which prison they might be sent to, they would be kept separate from the adult inmates.

On Friday, September 6, the jury in Alex and Derek's trial announced that they had reached a verdict. Almost immediately, Judge Bell ordered Chavis's jury to return to the courtroom as soon as possible. However, Bell decided to announce the verdict in Alex and Derek's trial first.

After deliberating for nearly five hours over two days, the jury found Alex and Derek King guilty of second-degree murder without a weapon. They had also found the boys guilty of arson.

When the verdict was announced, Alex's face remained expressionless. Derek merely bowed his head.

Kelly Marino wiped tears from her eyes and held her head in her hands.

By convicting the boys of the lesser offense, the jury spared them from mandatory life prison terms without the possibility of parole. As it was, the boys each faced sentences of 22 years to life in prison on the second-degree murder conviction, and up to 30 years on the arson conviction. Bell set their sentencing for October 17.

An hour later, after Chavis's jury had been brought back into the courtroom, Judge Bell opened the previously sealed verdict. He announced that Chavis had been acquitted of both the murder and arson charges. Chavis, "greatly relieved," according to his attorney, wiped tears from his eyes moments after the verdict was read.

Members of Terry King's family were shocked and angered by both verdicts, but particularly so over Chavis's acquittal. Greg King, Terry King's brother, said, "I'm disappointed to have the adult manipulator set free, yet have the abused children in prison.

"But that's our justice system," he added. "They [the boys] were devastated. The judgment was the first time they realized the weight of what was going on."

It was now Rimmer's turn to explain his strategy. "I felt there was enough circumstantial evidence that he [Chavis] motivated and influenced them [Alex and Derek]," he said. "I thought perhaps he encouraged them to do it, but I never felt Chavis was there. . . . The boys said he was the perpetrator, but the jury rejected their testimony. They didn't believe it. . . . The jury gave them every break they thought they could give them."

Rimmer took it a step further and said that the boys had been given a "jury pardon." He said that the jury knew that Terry King had been killed with a weapon, but had nonetheless come back with a verdict of second-degree murder "without a weapon."

"That's a jury pardon," Rimmer said. "That's okay, I don't have a problem with that."

However, when Rimmer's remarks got back to the King boys' jurors, the forewoman, Lynn Schwarz, 52, told reporters for the *Pensacola News Journal* that nothing could be further from the truth. None of the jurors, she said, believed that either of the boys had actually swung the bat that killed their father. Instead, she said, they believed that Chavis had com-

mitted the slaying. Schwarz said the jurors felt that
Alex's and Derek's confessions had sounded forced
and prepared, and that the panel had not believed
them. She said that the jurors were incredulous when
they learned that Chavis had been acquitted. "I was
so shocked," Schwarz said. "I just couldn't believe
it. . . . It's too bad they couldn't have all been tried
together. That might have been a fairer trial. . . . It's
disturbing that twelve people could see it one way
and six people another. But I don't blame that jury.
They saw a different presentation and a different in-
terpretation."

"When they asked Alex [on the taped interview]
about something he wasn't coached in," said Glenda
Berg, 51, another juror, "his voice changed and his
demeanor changed. It was almost like two different
people [talking]."

Jurors felt that the boys' confessions didn't sound
believable in part because they used terms like
"wooden structure" and "flammable material," terms
that seemed out of character and not typically part of
a child's vocabulary. Schwarz said that the jury felt
the detectives could have put more effort into the
investigation.

"Just as common men," Schwarz said, "we were
sitting there and listening to the confessions. There
were so many discrepancies between one boy and
another. And then there were some places where they
were exactly the same, the same verbiage. The investigators should have immediately said, 'There's a
problem here, and we've got to look into this more,
go back to the scene and try to corroborate some of
this.' But they didn't. It's like they just stopped with
the confessions."

Another juror, Mary Lupton, 29, citing the lack of physical evidence and the discrepancies in the boys' stories, said that the full details of what happened may never be learned. "There are so many things that are left unanswered," Lupton said. "Things that I would like to find out, but I don't think anybody will. Only they know truthfully what events really took place. Only them and God, and that will be their final judgment."

Schwarz said that the jury had decided to convict Alex and Derek of second-degree murder because they believed that the boys had opened the door or left it unlocked so that the killer could enter the house. Schwarz said the jury was uncertain about whether either Alex and Derek or Chavis had actually planned to kill Terry King ahead of time.

Alex and Derek "knew he was going to come in," Schwarz said. "But I don't think they really knew what he was going to do, or even if Chavis knew what he was going to do."

Schwarz said that during their deliberations, the jurors had wanted to see the photos of the bruises on Terry King's chest, but were denied the request.

"We thought Terry might have woken up when Chavis came in and had gone over to him," Schwarz said, describing one scenario the jury considered. "We thought Chavis might have hit him twice in the chest, knocking him back in the chair, before beating him on the head."

Now no one would ever know for certain.

"It's certainly sad," Rimmer said of the verdicts. "It's unfortunate, and there's really no winners. But the jury did the right thing, and I'm proud of them. . . . If they had believed the boys were telling the truth in court, they would have found Chavis guilty. . . . They [Alex and Derek] did do it, and a jury found that they did it."

Responding to accusations that two prosecutions on identical charges had been a legal travesty, both Rimmer and State Attorney Curtis Golden said that they were comfortable about their prosecutorial decisions. They also claimed that they never had two legal theories that they were pursuing. They had never thought that Chavis actually swung the bat that killed King, but had instead believed that Chavis had encouraged the boys to kill their father. Both Golden and Rimmer claimed they had always believed that Alex came up with the plan and that Derek committed the crime.

"Our theory was that Chavis was a principal in the first degree in that he encouraged the boys and gave them moral support," Golden said. "The theory was always that the boys were the perpetrators. Those theories are not inconsistent. We prosecute more than one person for a crime all the time."

Even though Chavis had been acquitted, both Golden and Rimmer expressed that they had been comfortable prosecuting him on the first-degree murder and arson charges, although both admitted that they would not have wanted a first-degree murder conviction against Chavis to prevail.

"If I had not brought first-degree murder charges against Chavis by bringing the boys before a grand jury and letting them tell their stories," Rimmer said, "what would people be saying now? They'd be saying Chavis did it, and why wasn't he charged?"

"If Chavis had been convicted," Golden said, "we

probably would have recommended that the judge set aside his conviction."

"The judge sits as a thirteenth juror," Rimmer added. "The judge can reweigh the evidence. If the evidence is insufficient despite the jury's verdict, he can overrule. It is kind of unusual, but there is case law on that."

"We felt like the right thing to do was to let it go to the jury first," Golden said. "But if the jury had convicted him, we would have asked the judge to review the evidence."

Some critics would later ask: What if the judge had refused to review the evidence? What if the case had involved the death penalty? Would the prosecutors have had the courage to stand up and try to undo an injustice? Or would they have let it go by the wayside?

CHAPTER 25

At the boys' sentencing on October 17, the case took yet another bizarre turn when Judge Bell announced that he would grant a motion filed by the boys' defense attorneys to throw out their convictions. Bell ordered the prosecutors and the defense attorneys to enter mediation to straighten out the case. If mediation talks failed, Bell said that he would order a new trial for the boys.

As basis for his decision, Bell cited the state's presentation of conflicting evidence regarding who actually wielded the bat in the two separate trials.

On the same date, Bell moved Rick Chavis's trial for lewd and lascivious acts against Alex King to February 10, 2003. Chavis's attorney, Michael Rollo, also sought and was granted a delay for Chavis's trial on charges of being an accessory after the fact to murder, and tampering with evidence. That trial was moved back to February 24, 2003. Rollo said that he needed additional time to prepare for those trials.

. . .

The fact that Alex and Derek's conviction had been thrown out by Judge Bell could mean that the boys would walk.

"There's definitely a very real possibility that they could get away with this now," Rimmer said. "The idea that the ones who committed the murder will go free always concerns me. But if that happens, I'll just have to suck it up. It's definitely discouraging, but I feel very good about how I handled the cases, because I let the juries hear the testimonies and decide on their own."

"That was the strangest roller coaster ride I've ever been on," said James Stokes, Alex's attorney. "Every time you think this case can't get any stranger, it does. I halfway expect the mediator's head to explode in the middle of the negotiations and aliens come out with the way the case has been going."

A number of people were saying that Bell had decided to throw out the boys' convictions because he had given in to public pressure.

"I've heard that," Stokes said, "and I've been telling those people, 'You don't know Frank Bell, do you?' It's not as though we have a bleeding-heart liberal judge here. He has no problem passing off thirty-year sentences. I think he just thought that this was something he couldn't let stand, and it took a whole lot of moral fiber to do it."

Bell appointed attorney Bill Eddens to mediate the case, possibly the first murder case in Florida history to go into mediation. Charles Cetti, a full-time mediator who has been practicing law for thirty-six years, hailed Bell's decision as a good one. Cetti said that it could set a precedent for judges to follow in future cases involving juveniles facing adult charges.

"A lot of eyes are going to be on this case to see whether or not it's going to work out," Cetti said. "What's the risk to the judge in ordering mediation? The worst that could happen is they don't settle in mediation and they go to appeals or a retrial. The best is they agree to a settlement and save a lot of time. As I view it, it's a riskless procedure."

"I hold out extreme hope that we can work this thing out and avoid another circus trial," Stokes said. "We'll just have to see what the state is willing to have the boys plead to . . . this seems to be the first time they've caught a break in about twelve or thirteen years."

"Terry's been forgotten in all this," said Wilbur King, Terry's father. "My son is gone, and while people say his boys didn't get justice, it's my son who didn't get justice. They aren't trying to find the killer of my son anymore. They are just trying to let those two boys off scot-free. . . . Terry had reached a goal he'd been trying a long time to attain, having a house for him and the boys. People picture these boys as angels, but Lucifer was an angel who turned against God, too. They were capable of doing this, I don't care how little or angelic they are. But I am not angry at the boys. I forgave them when they were first incarcerated. I said, 'Whether you did it or not, I'm here tonight to forgive you,' and before I left we had a prayer together."

As the mediation got under way, the circus calliope played in the distance as celebrity comedian Rosie O'Donnell hired Miami attorneys Jayne Weintraub and Ben Kuehne to represent the boys. According to her publicist, O'Donnell had been an abused child herself and had been following the plight of the King boys for months. However, because the case was in mediation and not in an appeals stage, it appeared doubtful that either of O'Donnell's attorneys would be very involved.

The boys' mother, Kelly Marino, said that she wanted Stokes, Potter and Corder off the case if mediation efforts failed and the case went back to court. "I like them personally," Marino said. "I think they're nice people, and I appreciate everything they've done. But from what I saw in the trial, I don't care for them as attorneys. Not in a murder trial. Maybe in something smaller, but not a murder trial with my boys." Instead, she said that she wanted Rosie O'Donnell's Miami attorneys on the case. "I'm not trying to make trouble," Marino said. "I'm just trying to do what's best for my children."

On Wednesday, November 14, all sides had announced that they had reached an agreement. Alex and Derek agreed to plead guilty to a reduced charge of third-degree murder and arson in connection with their father's slaying. Third-degree murder is defined as an unintentional killing that occurred while another felony crime was being committed.

"Certain felonies, like robbery, constitute first-degree murder," Rimmer explained. "But in this case the third-degree felony is battery, which is not in the listing of charges, that is, the beating death of Terry King with the bat. For third-degree murder, you only have to show that the defendant intended to commit the battery."

In entering his guilty plea, Derek King signed a statement, dated November 13, 2002. It read:

I, Derek Alan King, do hereby freely and voluntarily swear the following is true:

Rick Chavis encouraged my brother Alex and I to run away. He gave Alex $20 and two keys (a key to his fence and a key to his door) so that we could get into his house; Alex and I stayed at Rick's house until I was caught by the police in Pace. During that time Rick told us that we could stay with him forever; allowed us to skip school; allowed us to use marijuana; hid us when our dad came by so that we would not be caught; planted a fake call on his answering machine to make it look like we were not staying with him and played it to my dad; allowed us to stay up as late as we wanted; allowed me to smoke cigarettes; offered to have sex with me; spent a lot of time kissing Alex while Alex sat on his lap; offered to hide us from our dad until we turned 16 years old and could live where we wanted; told us that dad would kill us before he would let us live with Rick; told us that he might have to protect us from our dad; told us that our dad mentally abused Alex by "staring him down," which Rick said was extreme mental abuse.

On the night of my dad's death, Alex told me that Rick was going to come by and pick us up at midnight. Alex suggested that I kill dad. I murdered my dad with an aluminum baseball bat. I set the house on fire from my dad's bedroom. We went to the EZ Serve on the corner of Muscogee Road and called Rick, who came right away and picked us up. Rick drove us to a field just over the Alabama line and told us to take off our clothes. We rode in the trunk of his car in our underwear with the clothes to Rick's house. We rode in the trunk so nobody could see us.

We had done this before during the time we ran away.

We spent the next two days at Rick's house. While at Rick's house Rick washed our clothes as soon as we got to his house. That was Rick's idea. We smoked marijuana and slept in Rick's room the first night. Alex slept in Rick's bed and so did I. Rick started talking about what we should say to the police. He told us to say we killed our dad because dad abused us. This was not true. My dad never abused me. He told us to say the killing was in self-defense. He told us to lie and not tell the police about ever being at his house or his picking us up at the EZ Serve. He told us to tell the police we hitchhiked to Pace instead. We went over this many times until Rick was sure we would get it right. Rick then called Reggie Jernigan and turned us in to the police.

The first story we told the police was partially true; the rest was changed to protect Rick.

After Derek signed the document, attorneys Dennis Corder and Sharon Potter signed as witnesses.

Alex's signed, handwritten statement, also dated November 13, 2002, was entered as follows:

I met Rik when I was 7 years old. He was a friend of my dad. About 1 yrs. ago we began our relationship. We first had sex not long after my 12th birthday. Rik told me he loved me more than anyone else. Rik told me I could cum liv w/him if things got to bad w/my dad. Rik told me my dad wasn't my rel father. Rik gave me 20$ and told me if I ever neded to run away I should cum to liv w/him. Derek & I ran away & went to Rik's house. Rik hid us out &

told us we could liv w/him. Rik told me he love me.
Rik told me I was gay & only he understood me.
Rik took Derek over to Pace to visit his friend &
was caut. Rik told me he was afred of what my dad
would do to 3 of us if Derek said anything. Rik
droped me off w/my dad in Pace. When we got to
Mike Tie house we talked 'bout killin my dad. When
we got home Derek got bat and hit dad in hed. After
wile dad didnt mov. We set bedro. on fire. Then we
went to stor & cald Rik. Rik pikd us up. Rik took
us to feld & we put most clothes in trunk. Rik took
us to house. Rik calm us then smok pot w/us. Rik
& I & Dk went to bed. Next day we spend most in
basment hidin from cops. Rik say ple self D. Rik say
we cum liv w/him. Rik say dont talk bout him. Rik
say say we got in fit w/blood the skrashes on arm
from yard at dad. We told cop story. I suggested that
Derek kill my dad and that started a short talk about
it. (I don't remember what exactly was said).

Alex's signature appeared at the bottom of the
page, along with his attorney's signature as a witness.

It was never made clear whether Alex had deliberately written his statement with the misspellings
and abbreviations. But it seemed strange that he had
no difficulty completing the final sentence correctly.

Judge Bell sentenced Derek to eight years in
prison, and Alex to seven years. Bell gave the boys
credit for the time that they had already served in the
county jail. Both would be eligible for early release
after having served 85 percent of their sentences.

Meanwhile, in January 2003, Rick Chavis still
faced charges of kidnapping and sexual battery involving committing lewd or lascivious behavior, ac-

cessory after the fact of murder, and tampering with evidence. Chavis pleaded innocent to all charges.

Alex and Derek were expected to testify against Chavis at his trials. In the meantime Chavis remained incarcerated in the Escambia County Jail.

Following the holidays of 2002, and after rolling into the new year of 2003, Rick Chavis's trial for lewd and lascivious acts against Alex King got under way on Monday, February 10, again in Judge Frank Bell's courtroom. David Rimmer remained the prosecutor on the case, and Mike Rollo continued as Chavis's attorney.

Attorneys for both sides did not believe that jury selection would be easy. Many potential jurors claimed that they would likely find Chavis guilty because of his 1984 conviction on similar charges. However, by the end of the day, out of a jury pool of more than 100 people, the prosecution and defense lawyers managed to seat a six-person jury that consisted of two men and four women. There were also two alternates. The jurors consisted of two Navy men, an engineer, a court reporter, a shipyard worker and a postal service worker. Surprisingly, one of the jurors was chosen even though she said that she had been sexually molested when she was a child.

The next day Alex, his voice now growing deeper with the onset of puberty, again took the witness stand to testify against Rick Chavis. Following brief opening statements by each side, the jurors heard Alex describe how he and Chavis performed oral sex on one another during a five-month period in 2001. Alex testified that he and Chavis had performed oral sex on each other at five different locations: Chavis's bedroom, the back seat of an old junked car, Chavis's living room sofa, a tool shed, and inside a vacant home owned by Escambia County Sheriff's Deputy Reggie Jernigan. The boy said that the sexual encounters began shortly after he turned 12 on July 12, 2001, and ended three days before his father was murdered. It began when Chavis began telling the boys that Terry was not a good father to them.

"He would say bad things," Alex testified. "He would keep bringing up little things my dad did. He told me that my dad was mentally abusing us."

Alex told the jurors that he and his brother enjoyed being at Chavis's house because they were free to do whatever they wanted, like watching television and smoking marijuana whenever they felt like doing so.

"Was there anything Ricky Chavis would not let you do that you wanted to do?" Rimmer asked.

"No, sir," Alex responded. ". . . He said that he loved me. No one understands me like he did. We were different and both gay."

Alex took the jurors through the details of how Chavis had convinced him he was gay, and how Alex had responded in several handwritten love notes to Chavis. He said the sexual encounters began on the evening of his birthday when, after sitting on the patio awhile, the two of them moved to the sofa in Chavis's livingroom. Once on the sofa, Alex said, he and Chavis took off their clothes and proceeded to perform oral sex on each other. The sex continued in the various locations over the next five months, Alex said, and he and Chavis became more open about their relationship. There were instances, for example, where Alex would sit on Chavis's lap in front of

Derek, and the two would hold hands, rub each other, grab each other's private parts and French kiss. Alex said that he could only remember about nine incidents in which he and Chavis engaged in sex.

Under cross-examination, Rollo pointed out that Alex had previously stated that he recalled twenty sexual encounters with Chavis—but now he was saying that he remembered only about nine. Rollo made sure he emphasized the discrepancy to the jury. He also asked Alex if he could recollect the dates and other specifics about his sexual encounters with Chavis. Alex said that he could not—he could only recall where they took place. Many times throughout his testimony Alex seemed hesitant with his responses.

Rollo also asked Alex to describe the shape, size and appearance of Chavis's penis to the jury.

"I don't recall," Alex stated.

Rollo focused on the fact that Alex and Derek had changed their stories while in jail, and on the lies that they had admitted to. For example, their first version of the events surrounding their father's death was that they had committed the murder and that Chavis had not been involved. Then, while in the Escambia County Jail, they concocted a plan in which they would point the finger at Chavis. When they were ready with the plan they testified before a grand jury, in April 2002. When Rollo asked why he and Derek had changed their story and lied to the grand jury, only to later change their story and confess again that they had killed their father, Alex said they had done so because they were facing life in prison.

"If we were to tell the story Chavis told us to tell," Alex said, "we would get life."

When Rollo asked Alex if he and his brother had made up the details about Alex's sexual relationship with Chavis to make it appear that Chavis had a motive to kill their father, Alex responded: "I really do not recall why certain parts of the story were planned. Parts of it were true."

Did they kill their father? Rollo wanted to hear a response again, and get it on record once more.

"I sat on the couch," Alex stated in explaining their father's killing. "My brother got in front of him, then killed him with the baseball bat."

Additional witnesses who testified for the state included the boys' paternal grandmother, Joyce Tracy, who said that she had seen Alex come home with hickeys on his neck after visiting Chavis.

Linda Walker, Alex and Derek's maternal grandmother, testified how Chavis had told her on several occasions that he wanted to obtain legal custody of Alex.

"He told us that Terry was abusing the kids mentally and that he wanted me to figure out how I could get custody of Derek and he could get Alex," Walker testified. "It made me wonder why he wanted Alex."

One of the victims that Chavis had been convicted of molesting in 1984, now 32 years old, described how Chavis had seduced him and his cousin with marijuana, then molested them.

Yet another witness, Robert Smith, a convicted felon, testified that he had overheard Chavis talking to other inmates at Escambia County Jail about having had a sexual relationship with Alex.

"He was telling them that he slept with Alex King," Smith testified. "He said he loved him and would do anything for him."

At one point, Rimmer presented a photo of Alex, taken with a Polaroid camera, to the jury. The photo, Rimmer said, had been found on the headboard of Chavis's bed, and had been dated August 11, 2001. The prosecutor also brought out a letter to Chavis in which Alex had written, "I love Ricky Chavis so much."

Derek King took the stand as well, and testified that, while he did not know for certain that a sexual relationship had existed between his brother and Chavis, he had felt that things were strange between them when he witnessed them holding hands, Alex sitting on Chavis's lap as they French kissed and fondled each other's private parts. As Derek recounted what he had witnessed, an occasional gasp could be heard from the gallery.

After both sides rested, Rimmer presented his closing arguments. He focused on Alex's testimony in an attempt to convince the jury that it was credible, and asked them to use common sense in reaching their decision on whether to convict Chavis or not.

Rollo, on the other hand, focused his closing arguments on discrediting Alex's and Derek's testimony. He argued that if Chavis were convicted based on the lies that Alex and Derek had told, it would be a "perversion of American justice."

"Don't be like everyone else who has been deceived by Alex and Derek," Rollo told the jurors. "Don't add to their victim list. Their lies have caught up with them. Don't be fooled."

He pointed out how Alex had been unable to remember specifics about his alleged sexual encounters with Chavis, as well has his inability to recall details about Chavis's penis. He emphasized that Alex could only remember locations where the alleged acts occurred, not any dates or other specifics, except that the encounters had consisted of oral sex.

"It's one person's word against another," Rollo argued. "How easy is it for Alex to say he has sex with Ricky Chavis? Pretty easy. No date. No time. No month. No year. No summer. No fall. Nothing."

The jury deliberated for three hours, then returned to Judge Bell's courtroom. They found Chavis not guilty of sexually molesting and kidnapping Alex. They had, however, found him guilty of one count of the lesser charge of false imprisonment. Judge Bell immediately sentenced Chavis to 5 years in prison. Chavis clasped his hands together and smiled as the verdicts were read.

"Five years is very easy for me to impose," Bell told Chavis. "Extremely easy. By falsely imprisoning these two runaways, hiding them from their father and lying to him, that's unconscionable. That's lacking conscience."

"He's maintained all along that he never had any sexual contact with Alex," Rollo said after the verdict. "And I think the jury's verdict confirms that fact . . . we had a courageous jury, and it just shows that the jury system works."

Rimmer expressed disappointment at the jury's decision. "I thought I had enough compelling evidence to corroborate Alex's testimony, but I can't do anything about the fact that he and Derek told so many lies," Rimmer said. "You cannot make a silk purse out of a sow's ear . . . you get up, and you go on, and you keep fighting."

Rimmer said that he and Rollo had been discussing a possible plea agreement regarding Chavis's upcoming trial on charges of accessory after the fact to murder, and tampering with evidence. Now, however, despite the fact that Rollo still wanted to discuss a possible plea agreement, Rimmer said that it was no longer an option.

"The only plea agreement I would make with Mr. Chavis is that he can plead straight up and throw himself on the mercy of the court," Rimmer said. "But he'll probably miss. I will not give Chavis one scintilla, not the slightest deal of any kind. It's no deals."

Detective John Sanderson, who had been sitting in the rear of the courtroom when the verdicts were read, told reporters for the *Pensacola News Journal* that he was not surprised at the trial's outcome. He said that he had been convinced that Alex and Derek had killed their father from the beginning, but he had reservations regarding the boys' claims that Chavis had been engaged in a sexual relationship with Alex.

"The big problem here, to my mind, is the lack of credibility of the boys," Sanderson said. "Having worked this case from the beginning, seeing the way they act in different settings, seeing the way they react to different situations and then how they are in court, I personally have a problem with their credibility."

Family members, particularly Kelly Marino, were not pleased with the outcome of Chavis's trial on the sexual molestation and kidnapping charges. Marino was particularly critical of David Rimmer's prosecution of the case.

"This is a sad day for any child who has been sexually abused," Marino said. "People get more time for drug charges. I think Rimmer did a horrible job prosecuting the case. I think he did the bare minimum. He tried ten times harder to convict my children."

On Monday, March 3, 2003, this time in the courtroom of Escambia County Circuit Judge Joseph Tarbuck, Rick Chavis went on trial on charges of being an accessory after the fact to murder, and tampering with evidence. Like his previous trial, the proceedings would last barely two days, including the time it took to select a jury. After hearing evidence and testimony pertaining to how Chavis had picked up the boys at the convenience store across the road from their house immediately after Terry King's slaying, hiding them out afterward and initially lying to the police, and washing their clothes afterward, as well as other evidence and testimony that had previously been presented to show his involvement, the jury deliberated approximately five hours before coming back with their verdict.

On Wednesday, March 5, the jury announced that it had found Chavis guilty of both charges. Judge Tarbuck immediately sentenced him to 30 years in prison on the accessory after the fact to murder conviction and an additional 5 years on the tampering with evidence conviction. Tarbuck ordered both sentences to run concurrently. Under Florida law, Chavis must serve 85 percent of his sentence, 25½ years in this case, before becoming eligible for parole.

His attorney was outraged at the verdict and the judge's promptness in meting out the sentence. He was particularly incensed over the fact that Chavis's sentence amounted to more than four times the prison terms Alex and Derek had received for killing their father.

"It was a persecution, not a prosecution," Rollo said. "And it's been that way from the beginning. The jury spent five hours deliberating, and the judge took maybe fifteen seconds making up his sentencing decision. That was totally unfair. . . . if Mr. Chavis is the one orchestrating this tampering with evidence, if he's so bright, why wouldn't he have taken these clothes and burned them?"

Rollo vowed to file an appeal.

"None of this would have happened if it hadn't been for Chavis," Rimmer countered. "He was heavily involved with them, and his involvement is what led them to do what they did."

"Our kids have gotten their sentence, and it was time for Chavis to get his," Jimmy Walker, Alex and Derek's maternal step-grandfather said of the verdict. "Now he won't be able to hurt any more little boys."

"This is a happy ending to a very, very hard year-and-a-half," said Kelly Marino. "Hopefully, he'll be a very old man when he gets out." Marino said that she continues to believe that Chavis killed Terry King, not her boys.

"To be honest, I was worried," John Sanderson said as he waited in the courtroom to hear the verdict. "It's so unpredictable with a jury. So often you'll have juries that fall for the smoke screens of the defense. My only emotion was relief. Absolute relief. . . . I think it's all behind us now."

• • •

The Florida Department of Corrections transferred
Alex and Derek to the jurisdiction of the Department
of Juvenile Justice. As a result, Alex was sent to the
Okeechobee Juvenile Offender Correctional Center
and Derek was sent to the Omega Juvenile Prison to
complete their sentences.